P9-DCS-732

"What kin are we all to each other, anyway?"
AUNT MALLEY GANCHION

"JE est un autre." RIMBAUD

HOUSE OF BREATH

RANDOM HOUSE   •   BOOKWORKS

Copyright © 1949, 1950, 1975 by William Goyen
All rights reserved under International and Pan American
Copyright Conventions.

First printing January 1975   1,500 copies in cloth
                               7,500 copies in paperback

Illustration by Elizabeth Fairbanks
Typeset by Vera Allen Composition Service, Hayward, California
Printed and bound by The Colonial Press, Inc., Clinton, Mass.
  under the direction of Dean Ragland, Random House.

This book is co-published by   Random House Inc.
                                  201 East 50th Street
                                  New York, N. Y. 10022

                    and   The Bookworks
                                  2043 Francisco Street
                                  Berkeley, California 94709

Distributed in the United States by Random House Inc., and
simultaneously published in Canada by Random House of Canada
Ltd, Toronto.
Booksellers please order from Random House.

Sections of this novel have appeared in *Accent, Southwest Review,
Penguin New Writing, Partisan Review* and *Harper's Magazine.*

Library of Congress Cataloging in Publication Data

Goyen, William.
   The house of breath.

   "A Random House/Bookworks book."
   I. Title.
PZ3.G7484Ho4   [PS3513.097]   813'.5'4   74-23987
ISBN 0-394-49699-X
ISBN 0-394-73053-4 pbk.

Manufactured in the United States of America

THE AUTHOR wishes to acknowledge his gratitude to the editors of *The Southwest Review* for the Southwest Review Literary Fellowship awarded him in 1949 for work on this book.

For Frieda and Walter

Note on the Twenty-Fifth Anniversary of This Book

It is twenty-five years since this, the exultant song of my earlier days, elegy to my homesickness, memorial to my going-out, was first published.

I am pleased that this Second Edition will probably reach many new people; but most of all I could hope it would encourage young people to sing out of themselves their own music, to reveal long-kept secrets, to disclose hidden hurt, to make connections with their beginnings, to realize the extent of their relationships to their own at home and to the great mysterious world.

And to those I loved, living and dead, who surrounded the writing of this book, in Houston, Texas, in Dallas, Texas, in Portland, Oregon, in Napa, California, aboard an aircraft carrier in the South Pacific, in London, in El Prado, New Mexico, those who live in this book today as vividly as then: I salute you again and embrace you again, now as long ago: Walter and Frieda and Stephen and Dorothy and Bob Linscott and Margo and Liz Ann and Lon and Allen and Margaret . . . .

W.G.

New York City
March, 1975

THE HOUSE OF BREATH

Under All the Land Lies the Title

I . . . and then I walked
and walked in the rain that turned half into snow and I
was drenched and frozen; and walked upon a park that
seemed like the very pasture of Hell where there were
couples whispering in the shadows, all in some plot to
warm the world tonight, and I went into a public place
and saw annunciations drawn and written on the walls.
I came out and felt alone and lost in the world with no
home to go home to and felt robbed of everything I never
had but dreamt of and hoped to have; and mocked by
others' midnight victory and my own eternal failure, un-
named by nameless agony and stripped of all my history, I was betrayed again.

Yet on the walls of my brain, frescoes: the kneeling
balletic Angel holding a wand of vineleaves,
announcing; the agony in the garden; two naked lovers
turned out; and over the dome of my brain Creations
and Damnations, Judgments, Hells and Paradises (we

are carriers of lives and legends — who knows the unseen frescoes on the private walls of the skull?).

Then I was standing against the wet, cold wall of
this building in the park and I slid down against the wet
wall, wanting to die, squatting there in the dark. Faces
glided past me up above me under the rainstreaked
moon of a streetlight like prows of safe ships with somewhere to go — the rain on some was beautiful — and all
around me they were meeting in the park and walking
away under the dripping trees, figures were walking up
and down upon the sodden leaves, and in my spell I
thought, *they are all passing me by, and I sink down, way*
below the faces, prows of ships.

And then I heard the voices again *(Come home, the*
light's on, come on home, Ben Berryben. I'll be glad when
you've had enough and will come on home again, I'm so blue
and so upset, can hardly swallow water . . .) (Swimma-
a-a! Swimma -a-a-a! come in 'fore dark . . .) (rescue the
Perishing!) (Boy, Boy, come out to the woodshed I've got
somethin to show you, by gum . . .) (Draw me, draw me, I
will follow. . . . In all your sunshines if you can remember
one day any darkness, that will be me drawing you . . . I
have left Word in the darkness for you, the Word that was
my flesh (take that Wafer); all darkness proclaims my Word
– listen in the darkness and you will hear it.) and I melted
down like the gingerbread man that ran and ran and
melted as he ran. I began to name over and over in my
memory every beautiful and loved image I ever had, to

name and praise them over and over like a rosary, bead by bead, saying, Granny Ganchion, I touch you and name you; Folner, I touch you and name you, Aunty, Malley, Swimma, Boy, I touch you and name you and claim you all. It was like a procession through the rooms of the house, saying, now this is the hall and there is the bottled ship and the seashell, this is the breezeway, there is the well and here is the map in the kitchen and the watery mirror in which, behold, is my face, *me*, my face . . . . I cried out "O Charity!", so that those who heard me might have thought I was a beggar crying; and wanted to die . . . .

II

WHAT *is it the wind seeks,
sweeping among the leaves, prowling round and round this
house, knocking at the doors, and wailing in the shutters?*

O Charity! Every frozen morning for awhile in early
winter you had a thin little winter moon slung like a slice
of a silver Rocky Ford cantaloupe over the sawmill; and
then I would go out to the well in the yard and snap off
the silver thorns of ice from the pump muzzle and jack
up the morning water and stand and look over across the
fairy fields at you where you lay like a storybook town,
and know that on all the little wooden roofs of houses
there was a delicate trail of lacelike rime on the shingles.
Then all the chickens and guineas of Charity would be
crowing and calling and all the cattle lowing, and the
Charity dogs barking (all with a sound that china
animals might make if they could crow or call or low),
and in that crystal and moonhaunted moment I would
stand, dazzling in the first sunray of morning, and won-

der what would ever happen to us all.

And on a spring Saturday you would be sitting there in your place in Texas "grinnin like a Chessy Cat" as Aunty said, so happy and hopping with all the people come in from the fields and farms to handle you and claim you and gather round in you — there was Glee Ramey and there was Sweet Climpkins and Sing Stovall and Ola Stokes, the music teacher ("One day a little bubble will break in your throat, honey, and then you'll have a beautiful voice. Just wait for the little bubble."), and all the Grants, who had to ford White Rock Creek to get in from their blackland farm — and families all standing together here and there or carrying out oats and feed and cartons of Pet's Milk from the Commissary.

And in the still, clear dusks I remember especially a voice that sounded in you, Charity, resounding as in a cistern, calling "Swimma -a-a! Swimma -a-a-a! Come in 'fore dark!" — Aunty calling Sue Emma, my cousin and her daughter (no voice calling this name can ever call back Sue Emma to that fallen splendid house, and it grows dark. But Sue Emma, dancing or hunching in the dark, grinding in her own glitter's ashes, might hear a calling voice within her that does not answer back). All my life since, in any place and for no reason at all, sometimes at dusk I will suddenly hear a voice calling "Swimma -a-a! Swimma -a-a-a! Come in 'fore dark!"; and wish we were all together in Charity again.

You had a little patch of woods behind the house that I remember. It had bearded trees that clicked and ticked and cracked and cheeped and twittered and lichen grew on an ancient fence like an old old sheep's coat; and stroking it with my hand once made me feel how old and lusterless and napworn you might be, Charity, and all the people in you, just as Aunty said. But to see an old live oak drop a single young little leaf twinkling to the ground was to know that there was still the shining new thing of myself in the world and I would be filled with some passion for something, bigger than Aunty's hopelessness, bigger than Granny Ganchion's agony, than all Charity — until suddenly I would hear the groaning of the cisternwheel back at the house, calling me back, and I would go.

You were such a place of leaves, Charity; and I think the first time I was ever aware of you as any place in the world was in a deep and sad and heavy autumn. Then you seemed to have been built of leaf and twig and bark, as a bird's nest is woven and thatched together, and had been used and used until you were withered; then you were shaken and thrown down into these ruins. All the summer of anything that had ever touched or known you seemed despoiled and was rubble that autumn, and I suddenly knew myself as something, moving and turning among these remnants. (Oh all the leaves I have known in you, Charity! — the shining leathery castorbean leaves, with the chickens cool under

them in the summer or sheltered from the rain (oh the
sound of the rain on the castorbean leaves, how forever
after Folner's funeral that sound reminded me of the funeral).) And the lace and grace of chinaberry leaves in a
summer breeze; and those of the vines that had a name I
did not know and hung, full of bees or busy humming-
birds all after the little sweet white bloom on it, over the
long front gallery of the house. Then of course the live-
oak leaves, that were flaked over Charity Riverbottom;
and muscadine leaves and sycamore leaves and the
leaves on go-to-sleep flowers. (In the autumn of one
year, every leaf that had ever hung on any Charity tree in
spring and summer lay fallen upon the ground and I
moved and turned through the wreckage like an unhung
leaf that would not lie down nor wither.)

In you, Charity, there stands now, as in the globed
world of my memory there glimmers the frosted image
of it, blown by all these breaths, the fallen splendid
house, sitting on the rising piece of land, out of which all
who lived and lost in it have gone, being dispossessed of
it: by death, by wandering, by turning away. And the
house appears, now, to be an old old monument in an
agony of memory of us, its ruined friezes of remains, full
of our speech, holding our things that speak out after us
as they once spoke into us, and waiting for one of us to
give it back its language and so find his own. (But I think
how our worlds — like this house — hold us within
them like an idea they might be having or like dreams

they are dreaming, where our faces are unreal, worn blurred stone faces of ancient metopes of kin, caught in soundless shapes of tumult, wrestling with invasion of some haunted demon race, half-animal, half-angel — O agony of faces without features like faces in fogs of dreams of sorrow and horror, worn holes of mouths opened, calling cries that cannot be heard, saying what words, what choked names of breath that must be heard) And to find out what we are, we must enter back into the ideas and the dreams of worlds that bore and dreamt us and there find, waiting within worn mouths, the speech that is ours. For now in this autumn when all the young are ceaselessly walking up and down under the falling trees, trying to make themselves real, I have walked and walked among the leaves that lie like lost claws clutching the earth that fed them, weaving and winding myself to myself, binding the lost leaf back to the tree. For all that is lost yearns to be found again, re-made and given back through the finder to itself, speech found for what is not spoken.

III

TO GET TO the house,
Charity, if I had been in town, I would just start walking
toward the sawmill, down Main Street (which was really
only the Highway named this for the short time it ran
through you and became a little piece of you) under all
the Charity trees. I would pass the only stores you had,
looking across Main Street at each other; and ahead of
me would stretch the Highway, going to pretty close
little towns like Lufkin and Lovelady, and behind me it
wound to faraway places, huge and full of many people,
like Dallas or Santone. Then I would turn off at the twisted cedar, in whose branches I had been as often as any
bird, that had a forked limb like a chicken's wishbone,
where once I slipped and hung like Absalom until Mrs.
Tanner came running to save me; then there would be
the sawmill, where my father worked (the men
urinating in the lumberstacks) — and came home with
sawdust in his pockets and shoes — that had a long,

legged sawdust conveyor sitting like a praying mantis. And next would come the graveyard, nothing but names and dates and enormous grasshoppers vaulting over the graves; and the little Negro shacks next, with black faces at the windows or some good old Negro sitting on his front gallery or calling to little Negro children playing in the mudpuddles, and a rooster crowing somewhere, after the rain. Finally I would take the sandy road, my feet barefooted and glad in it, stand by the Grace Methodist Church where it always seemed I could hear the voice of Brother Ramsey inside saying "Blessed are the peacemakers, for they are the children of God," and then if I suddenly looked up, after thinking into the sand what peacemakers were, I would see the house, looking at me like a face of a sleeping bird (the cisternwheel would be its tail over it), and calling me back to it, home.

It was a big, wide, live house with a long hall running right through the middle of it, and had many people in it, Aunty, Uncle Jimbob, Aunt Malley, Uncle Walter Warren, Christy, Granny Ganchion and all the cousins, little and big: Swimma, Follie, Berryben, Jessy, Maidie and all — even Miss Hattie Clegg, who came to live with us. There was always that wagon in the field; it had lost a wheel and was standing broken at the back and wrenched to one side. A family of chipmunks lived and bred and lived on in it. Close to the outdoor well was the babybuggy, ragged and decrepit, like the sloughed-off husk of abandoned infancy, in which many babies had been fitted and ridden round; and later, when there were no more babies in the house, the children who had lain in it had played with it, recklessly, as if disdainful of any infancy, until Aunty had captured it again and planted some Hen-and-Chickens in it. If it was winter, the cattle would be standing in a stare in the fields, dull and motionless; and the ragged hens would be huddled drooping by the barn. Then it seemed that summer might not ever come again (and Jessy played her jacks in the hall or sang for one of her sick dolls, "Mama, Mama, I am sick, run for the doctor quick quick quick!"; and I gazed at the picture of the sorrowful girl sitting playing her lyre on the side of the world). But summer or winter, turning and turning over it all like a blessing or a curse (or sometimes blowing as if it were trying to blow the house down) was the whirling wheel at the cistern.

You had other places, Charity — the little Bijou (said "Byejo" by everybody) Theatre, bright and rowdy, where Jack Norbitt played, thumping his wooden leg, the piano for the show — mostly one piece called "Whispering," over and over again. And you had the City Hotel — but that burned and brought all Charity to it in nightgowns and out of its wreckage they carried an old charred drummer burned in the praying shape they found him in — and I would never go this way to town again, to smell the rain on burnt woodash and flesh. Then there was the Postoffice, where the faces of Sam and Birdie and old Bill Grady were framed in each win-

dow like a mantel array of family photographs as I
passed, going to get the mail. And there was the Racket
Store and Sam Brown's Dry Goods Store that had the
smell of cretonne and gingham and Union Jack overalls
in it, and old Mrs. Huffman with a pair of scissors hanging on a black ribbon round her neck saying, "Kin I hep
ye, Boy Ganchion?".

   All these years, Charity, that I was in you, crystal
dazzling in the radiant shell of mornings, eye going over
and over you, reflecting everything and wondering, I
never said anything, but only waited for some speech
that the breath of the house was breathing into me. In
memory the image of these days in you is what happened once on Main Street when a bunch of boys was
standing round telling about things and suddenly one of
them pointed out of the circle and called, "Look! Standin
there listenin with's mouth open!" and they all looked
and laughed. It was me, suddenly aware of myself looking, that they were pointing and laughing at; and I went
on away, then, thinking, 'I'll go home to the house; I
have a place to go.' For there was not a thing to say.

   Within the house you held, Charity, and in the hall
that led to the breezeway there lay, propping open the
door to the breezeway in summer and, cold to touch and
of no use at all in the corner in winter, the seashell that
Swimma brought. When she came running home the
time she thought oil was on the property she brought it

as a present from Florida to her mother, Aunty. On it was written PLAYGROUND OF THE WORLD. This was all she ever gave her mother.

Summer and winter, doorstop or just seashell, it always had the little roar of the sea in it. Sometimes I found Aunty sitting with it at her ear and once I saw Christy whisper into it; and one of the few words he ever said to me was when he held it out to me once and said "Listen!"

(One time when Swimma was in high school I saw Aunty after her because Swimma had a note in her hands that she wouldn't let Aunty see. They ran out of Aunty's room through the hall and onto the breezeway, Swimma yelling, "It's none of your business what I have or do!" and Swimma ran to the well and threw the note in. Then she had her tantrum and ran out into the yard, chickens shooting up frightened everywhere, feathers flying, and Swimma seemed like one of them; and she stayed away all afternoon. She came back late, from town where she had been, and Aunty looked out to see her coming and said, "Well yonder comes Miss Priss; I vow to you I don't know what we're goin to do with her."

Swimma prissed in home, through the gate, with her lipstick on and walking as if she had on highheels, and said to Aunty on the gallery, "I hoped you'd thought I'd run away, is what I'll do one day, too, sure's Satan."

Then she came in and sat on the bench in the hall

and gazed at herself in her mirror, making kissing shapes with her lipsticked lips and doing her lips around as if she were saying "ooooo!" and rocking her head as if she were whispering "hotcha!" — a word she was always saying around the house, now. She all of a sudden got mad as a bull and threw her mirror on the floor and broke it into pieces there where the seashell lay after she brought it, yelling, "Why do I have to have this nose as long as a pineywoods rooter's — and with a possible wart comin like Mama's? Dang it I wish I had the gold earrings Eulaly Sanderson has on in town today, and all the money they cost, and *she* was goin to have a wart on *her* nose!"

Aunty just got up from her chair on the gallery and said in at the front door, "Seven years bad luck little feist," for the broken mirror. (Oh she had it, seven and more.))

There also lay in the hall, close to the seashell door-stop, a pale green turpentine bottle with a perfect little ship in it that Christy made one winter (what was this man who made it?).

And in the hall there hung a picture of a blinded girl with a lyre, sitting on top of a blue, rolling world and bent over in some sorrowful, lyrical telling-out of a memory. When I looked at this picture, it seemed that some voice in me was telling out a memory of the world, as though I had always known the world, in what past of

mine, what dream? I stood and looked and heard the
song of the world that told of the splendor of itself, like
an object created by all that happened in it, and of what
was done in it through all its years: it sang out, in a voice
like Jessy's, frail and trembling, of fallings of angels,
down from a red raging heaven like falling birds or
leaves or dropped flowers; of the first man and woman
naked and yawning in a garden, their flesh speaking (O
for some intimacy of bodies speaking to each other,
creating a language for the first time that would be the
speech of all love in all the years — one simple sentence
of touch and burst) a language that would create and
speak out into the world all passion and all despair,
loneliness for lack of it that would be a kind of dumbness
of speech — where there is no love there is no speech —
and desire like speech unheard, and ecstasy like the
murmuring and pouring out of the sentence, bring body
to body and start a ceaseless murmuring, the turning of
the wheel of blood, yearning and tiring and yearning
again, eternally rising and falling. And the song sang of
kings and falls of kings, and plots of princes; princesses
in grated towers and queens in love or sending out ships
or causing battles for nations, and conquests of religions
and building of stained jewels of churches; of classes,
riots and clashes of classes, and systems discovered by
one man for all ages, and laws and pacts and edicts. The
singing was of architecture of great stone buildings
standing in light and throwing down their shadows

across swept spacious plazas, and of figures on the capi-
tals of columns — doves and granite grapes and tongued
gargoyles; of painted and striped baubles of cities, glittering with loot of robbed wealth, built over water, built
on mountainsides; of palaces and great dynastic houses
and fortifications and monasteries . . .

And over all this tumult of concourse of men alive
in the years of the world had hung the same old sky as
over you, Charity, with all the stories of stars in the con-
stellations: Orion hunting eternally through the frozen
wastes and ices of the bottomlands of the firmament, the
lights twinkling round his loins and girdling them,
Bulls; and Fishes; the Seven Sisters coming up,
clustered, like slow shot Roman Candle stars over Rob
Hill (just over there!), a thrown moon over like a
gleaming skull from the graveyard of centuries of moons
(thrown by what gravedigger's hand?) or sometimes like
the head of a laughing boy or a luminous fingernail-end
of some moving pointing finger.

In the kitchen, tacked on the wall by Christy, was a
map of the world. Christy often sat at night (and I sometimes with him) and looked and looked at the map,
almost as if he were talking to the world and adoring the
world and taking each part of it into himself as he
looked. Sometimes he showed me that by looking a long
time at the map and then closing your eyes, you could
open them again and look out into Bailey's Pasture and

see there, radiant and throbbing, the lighted shape of
the world. And sometimes it seemed on the map, as we
looked, that the whole world was melting down and
leaving drippings of the world on the map like melting
ice on a floor. Then the world was melting down into me
and into Christy and we were changed into the world. In
the enormous fluid of universe, ice floes of countries
were broken off and floating and Christy and I were
floating like separate (but bridged by some secret underwater island) lands. We saw together the brainshaped
countries and livershaped countries where the whole
mapped world looked like blooded lights of the dis-
sected, opened out and pinned down body of the world
as if it were an enormous fowl; and then we saw green
and orange seas with pearl chains of islands, and fringed
coasts. And we felt the wealth of nations, of colored pop-
ulations inhabiting like flocks of flowers — yellow or
black or red — the fields of countries; of wars and cru-
sades, of all the languages speaking to one another; and
we saw places with rivers and named after the rivers;
and we knew that there were many countries and lands
and that some, in the running out of many years ("The
years! the years!" Christy would whisper) would famish
and grow so used that ancient grapevines would not
give one more grape, and die — but that then other
countries, heretofore forest full of eyes and calls and
beaks against bark, and fat breasts of unshot birds, and
where cones lay like fruit and spores dropped and high

high grasses shone in sunlight; and floored with fresh soil ripe for roots and seeds in fields where seeds flew in the winds or were carried on hooves or tails or manes and dropped and watered by rains, planted and cultivated by no man; where airs were full of flying seeds and pollen and wings — but other countries then would be found (men see them from a peak, after long guessings of travelings; or from a wide and brimming river which they had opened like a marriage with the curved prow of their ship named after Queens and sent by Queens) and history go on. History got onto maps, Christy's gaze said, because men searched and because men were lonely and because men wandered and found countries and brought, like bees or winds or hairy carriers, the seeds *home:* in a box a tender frond in its soil, to be smoked or its fruit eaten; a leaf, a dried blossom; or rock-embedded ores; or in a bottle water from a lake or a spring; or cages of colored birds, a chained, aghast black man; or teeth or tusks; or a purse of precious stones.

Here, tacked on this wall in the kitchen of the house you held, Charity, was the world's body showing all the life in it; and all the life was in Christy and me — and our skulls became lighted globes of the world, that the map had stamped there, which each of us held in his hands, turning it round to find the worlds that each of us had given to the other.

IV

WHEN I FIRST discovered your River, Charity, I had the song of the world sung into me by the map and the picture and, looking at the river, map and picture and river were singing together the same story, of beginnings, and ages, and of movement through ages *towards* something, towards *me*. You had this little river, Charity, that scalloped round your hem like a taffeta ruffle. It glided through your bottomlands (that could be seen from the gallery of the house) winking with minnows and riverflies and waterbugs. It was ornamented with big, drowsy snapturtles sitting like figurines on rocks; had little jeweled perch in it and thick purple catfish shining in it and sliding cottonmouth watermoccasins. It crawled, croaking with bullfrogs and ticking and sucking and clucking and shining, round through meadows of bottomland palmettos (fanning in a breeze like a meadow of Methodist

women in July Prayer Meeting), between muscadine
vines that plashed up like fretted fountains (and trailed
and curled and twined over the ground and crept over
old stony logs and ancient saffron-golden rotted wood
festered with the decoration of pink and white and azure
fungusflowers, and climbed up trees and coiled round
their branches and then were flung down again in
tassels and sprays and thick swags over the river), under
purple hangings of moss and under bridges of many
little towns until, somewhere far away from you,
Charity, in a place you did not know but only imagined,
it swam into a bay.

O River! You were our Time flowing wrinkled and
ceaseless over stones and roots, sliming or mossing or
eroding them as Time passes over people and their
houses and objects, touching them with a ghostly in-
visible hand and changing them — see its work on the
the face, the hair, the body: mossing and wrinkling and
eroding. You were a kind of Beulah Land for everybody:
people gathered at you, gathering at water like creatures. You were known to be treacherous after rains and
in your deep places, where it was quietest, were dread
suckholes sometimes marked by the warning of a whirl-
pool, but not always. For a fording wagon full of the
Chubbs from Elmina had sunk into one of them and all
were drowned and people all along in the towns of
Onalaska and Pointblank and Camilla found bodies
coming along, now of the baby, now of Ora Bee Chubb,

now of the two boys, floating by; and although they waited and watched for Selmers Chubb, he never passed and it was guessed that he was caught in a snag. Others drowned in you, too — three Charity girls almost did while wading and squealing and one of them did and this was Otey Bell, rescued by Christy Ganchion, but too late. They rolled her over a log but she was drowned.

You had live bodies of bathers jumping in you in the summers; and waders; and seiners and rowers.

If somebody stood looking at his image in you, River, his head would seem to be a black flame or a black torch, furling and unfurling.

You seemed wicked, too, for once, on a fishing trip with some uncles and other men, I had lain listening all night to a conversation against the stitching call of katydids about women and certain Charity women; and then one man had said (it was Christy, my uncle) while he thought I was asleep, that he wondered if I had any hairs down there yet and drank his homebrew and said let's wake him up to see, and chuckled. I had lain trembling and waiting for them to come, knowing they would find what they came to see, quite a few, and lovely golden down, and they had been my secret; but they never came, only made me feel a guilt for secrets.

And you could make one feel terror, River; for men, as men will in any place at times, had turned suddenly hostile towards men along your moist sides, on hunting

trips, and no one seemed to have a friend among the
hunters — like the time of the hunting trip that I was
forced to go on and was almost shot because I had
cracked a pecan off to myself in the woods, standing in
the lemongreen light of trees, and the hunters had crept
upon me and aimed at the cracking noise I made, like a
squirrel they hunted, and would have shot if I had not
emerged just at the moment from the thicket and looked,
pitiful and pitifully, at them. Then they cursed and
turned upon me and turned upon each other because
they were tired and a bit drunk and the sun was hot and
there was a boy who did not want to hunt, not even to
shoot his niggershooter, but only crack his nuts, alone,
and foil them.

You had spectral pools standing still close to you,
full of their secret life, like your hidden otherlife —
ringed in November by gray, luminous trees whose
wiry branches were like tangled strands of steel; and
mauve and amber and russet ferns shimmered in the
phosphorescent marshes around. And in some trees sat
haunted, colored birds.

In summer the rich pond water was a vat of ripe
simmering fruit, of varnish color: golden in the sun,
holding like a rich syrup all the stock and plankton of the
woods: loam-wealth, growth richness, leaf and sap
goodness, the potlikker of the secret woods — all untouched and rare and gamy. There lolled fat, torpid, safe
fish, bobbling languorously over in the thick piny

syrup, bubbling their rubbery globules, like plump ripe fruit in their juices. Then the summer deep green growth of enormous ferns, dropping their quiet spores beneath themselves, and brambled, locked berrybushes with swollen, flaming berries, safe again, except from beak and tooth; and mayhaw and muscadine vines and ambushed snakes lying hot-bodied and dozing, their fluent eyes the mirrors of berry and frond and water-sparkle, or slipping through the maidenhair. There also were unanxious frogs with half-closed eyes and throbbing throats; and the noise of the heat in the steaming woods was a kind of heart-sound or a breathing sound; and there was the gasping of crickets.

But in the deep winter the brown Indian skin of ice lay over the pond and a bird might walk on the water like an apostle.

Yet they said that the Devil walked in the bottomlands.

In your bottomlands, which you kept moist and lush (except in droughts that dried you up and shamefully showed your white fishbelly of muscled sand and your green rippled ribs of shining treeroots), there lived a bunch of Negroes and they were called the Riverbottom Nigras. Your Riverbottom Nigras lived in little shotgun houses with a clappety porch and a swept dirt yard and a flowerbed neat as a flowered bonnet, bordered with green and amber bottles or fruitjars. They

grew some vegetables — you could see the tincans over
the tomato plants in the spring — and some of them
worked across at the Fuller's Earth Mill or the women
came to Charity houses and washed and ironed the
Charity clothes. But a lot of them mostly just fished in
you. Nearly every year you rose up, swollen with the
rains, and slid out to the Negroes' places to flood them
out, ruined their vegetables and rotted their porches and
twisted their steps; but your Riverbottom Nigras waited
until you shrank back into your bed, pulling their vegetables back with you and scattering the fruitjars and
cans, and then they went quietly back and cleaned up
your rivermess and leavings and made their places nice
again.

Your Nigras knew your bottomlands like their own
rooms, knew your good fishing places and where there
was white sand and safe hiding places for escaped con-
victs from Huntsville. They knew when mosquitoes
were coming, by wind or lack of wind, and when
rattlesnakes sloughed or were abroad. The Riverbottom
Nigras had lost children in you, caught on fishhooks
strange monsters from you that were sent by the Devil,
bathed in you and sung along you. Lovers had met in
your bottomlands, crapshooters snapped fingers
around a secret fire, and killers had run to you and lain
all night in some dense rushes where the Ku Klux might
not find them.

Yet above your bottomlands, River, like a hill of terror, rose Rob Hill in its shaggy old pelt of scrub oak and crowned by burning crosses, where the Ku Klux Klan met and burned a Negro to remind them all along you that they were Negroes.

You were my first river in the country of childhood and when I discovered you, from a hill in a blue, early morning, I saw you whispering along through the woods like the long and weaving *Märchen* of the woods murmuring history. Think of me then (was what you were singing) when I had never had a boat upon me or any net thrown or seine dipped into me, flowing only with moonlight or sunlight and all my swimming and breathing things within my womb (and such a thing as Charity never existed); and of my floods which I had (and caused no dikes to be made nor any human alarm, only the terror of creatures who knew the visits, and endured them, of catastrophe and built rushnests again, afterwards, moved eggs in time or their young away), rolling over on to the bottomlands where I lay heavy and large and pressing upon them. And then when it was time, folded back again over upon myself, a shrunken, lighter lover, and fell back to my size and place and ran on again, in repose, to my bay. What I left upon the bottomlands all could see — I left my sand in bars and wrote my designs and crystal shapes upon them and then birds' feet made their marks with mine and paws of

animals theirs and snakes made smooth, crooked,
wiped places with their bellies (what man first found
these and asked me what they meant?) and what I left on
the bottomlands anyone could have; but I fertilized the
land with my sperm of fishes' bones and algae and left
crawfish and swollen rats and wooden cattle and all my
lavish and manifold plankton, my mulch. Everything
flows into everything and carries with it and within it all
lives of its life and others' life and all is a murmuring and
whispering of things changing into each other, breed-
ing and searching and reaching and withdrawing and
dying. Whatever crossing is made each over other, by
boat or bridge or swimming, is to another side; and
whatever drowning is dying and sinking back into a
womb, and what salvation or rescue of the perishing in
waters or wickedness, dead or alive, is a union, of silence or rejoicing; and to drop down into any of us, into
depths (in river or self or well or cellar) is to lower into
sorrow and truth. But we are purged, to plunge beneath
a flood is to lose all guilty stains and to rise is to be
purified. And we are to keep turning the wheels we
turn, we are wind we are water we are yearning; we are
to keep rising and falling, hovering at our own marks,
then falling, then rising. (Who can set a mark or measure
us? They cannot name my tides or measure me by the
marks drawn on a wall; I hover.)

But let me tell you that if there is a call from the other
side, then come over, Red Rover, come over, over . . .

You came, young boy from the House, to these
woods with me running in them and you called out any
name (and I will never tell it) and the woods held the
name you called and trembled with the name and all the
nests shook with it and berries swung with the calling
like little bells, and flowers rocked the name like listening faces turning their ears to hear the name, and birds
flushed up at the calling of the name; and animals
stopped where they were going and pricked their ears
and heard and their ears held the name you called. You
walked and thought of all those killed by their love and
lovers, and you had none, of all lost causes of hunters
and explorers, of all failures of men going after something, and said the words that the Mexicans say, *O Díos,
O Díos, O Díos,* and wished and yearned for someone to
lead you and to follow. And you knew that I, river, had
gone out onto the land, the land of widespread corruption and drouth, the flaccid land of the dead, and lain
upon it and covered it with my sperm and brought up
life from corruption; that I crossed over my banks and
went where there was nothing of me, where I was not,
and left some of myself there. But there is the inevitable
return, we are forever going out and coming in, joining
and abandoning, alone and together.

Once, when you were swimming, naked, it happened for the first time to you in me. Christy stood on
the bank and told you and Berryben to jump in and
touch my bottom and see who could come up to the top

first; and you were struggling to come up first, rising
rising rising, faster, faster, when some marvelous thing
that can happen to all of us happened to you, wound up
and burst and hurt you, hurt you and you came up,
changed, last to the top trembling and exhausted and sat
down on my banks in a spell; and had lost (Christy
knew, and tried to make you jump into me again). You
blamed it secretly on Christy, that he had made you feel
like this, and were afraid of him for it. This was the way
you learned what could happen to you, but not why; like
a clock that could wind up and chime in you down there.

By me, in these woods, you once made up for what
you never had, played your fingers over my hairy rock-
moss and lay against my sandstone and ached and
cramped and burned and I know what happened there.
Just you hard against my rock; and in your trousers, all
over you, hot and running like glue — you washed you
in my waters; and by my waters you lay down and wept,
and slept, by me. From then on you were aware of the
feeling water could make you have, O we were lovers, I
had you rising and falling in me and you left something
in me and it was mixed with my rich sediment and my
spume, O we were lovers; and I cast your sperm mixed
in my spume and sediment onto the land, the country of
your beginnings, and we made it rich. What I taught you
is that there must be a rising and a falling, a bursting and
a casting out. All your family feared water, would not

cross it on bridges, would not swim much in it (but one drowned in it): cross it, love it, *be* water, you are river, I am you.

And once, in my greatest flood when I was swollen huge and throbbing with all my fluid, I crept through Charity and through Bailey's Pasture close to you and to your house and lay by you and by the house (O we were joined again) and heard within it all the murmurings of the house, by the shuttered window, in the cellar, in the loft, in the kitchen by the map, and sang my duet with the girl on the world; and you slipped out to me and dropped into me Swimma's seashell and Christy's ship in the bottle that I floated down and away onto the waters of the mapped world he looked at and became, and also dropped some Folner spangles and a stranger's photograph and a string of ruby beads — and I received them all and mixed them in my substance, in my stuff. And I lay upon all the life of the people of the house left in the pasture: the sawdust, the bones of frozen and shot Roma the cow, the go-to-sleep flowers, the bitterweeds, the lost doll, the babybuggy; I washed over all the footprints on the path of Folner and you and Berryben and Christy and Swimma; saw Malley peeking at me through the shutter and watched all of you sitting on the front gallery together fearing me; heard the grinding of the cisternwheel and heard the splashing of the dropped bucket in the well. And when I left the pasture you know what I left: what you left in me and I brought back to you and to your pasture, O we were lovers in your place and in my place, in bottomland and pasture.

And I knew your agony with Christy in my woods, heard it and took the gift of birds you threw me, Christy's yoke and your yoke and my yoke, and dissolved them in my substance.

O when I rolled over onto the world in my agony and thought, lost in Charity, that I might never find my way back home to the bottomlands, I slept by you; and in my agony I was reaching out to touch the world and I touched you when I touched the world, I touched myself that I had put in you. Reach, spread, roll out onto the world and touch, O Boy! O River!

When Christy and I looked at the map and saw all the life of the shaped countries, our minds were blown globes like the world and within the worlds of our minds there was created, mapped and carried there our idea of World and of History, although we were of little Charity; and our hearts, like a Creator, pumped all the creation: in *Märchen* and epic and *lieder* of blood: through the corridors of our veins, singing like troubadours and minnesingers and bards Iliads and Eddas, Odysseys and Geneses, and breaking echoes of history and time and the rabbled glory of men and life through ages in the spaces of our minds' universe — and creating everything again.

And hearing the blinded girl's song of the world in

the hallway, I melted into the world and changed into everything that had ever been created or constructed, buildings, woods, rivers, pomp, love, history; and everything entered into me, all involved in all.

You, River, then, held like a capsule of sperm the whole seed of creation; and the house we came from, breath breathed into it, like one uttered breath all the speech and all the life of men in a world of worlds.

But even a river, River, can fall to ruin (you lie so thin and weak and old). In time, important men came advising the Riverbottom Nigras that the land was bought and to move; and in time the bottomlands where, it seemed, Nigras and Charity gatherers were gathered so often, like a flight of summer flies that have vanished, were cleaned smooth as desert of palmettos and muscadines, and oilwells stood up over broken yellow swords, and you were turned out of your path as though you had forgotten all the ways you had ever gone and moved farther over into Riverside, white Fuller's Earth Mill on one side, gasping the white fogged breath; and on the other the black towers of riggings and the scraped and bald desert of yellowgreen or black slag, ugly subterranean rocks and the thick mudflats and slues like the slime of decomposition.

But across the icebound bottomlands, over the sleeted slues and the rime of the bog, with beak of horn and horned nails, chiming his terrible Midnight, stalks the bird whose ghost you are, O river O my waters.

It seems, Charity, that the young ones were always packing their suitcases to come back to you or to leave you again and the old ones sitting and waiting, taking the young ones back and keeping them as long as they could — they at their standoffish distance of never belonging there or anywhere that broke the old ones' hearts who never said a brokenhearted word — till they had to stand on the front porch again and watch them, the Folners and the Berrybens and the Sue Emmas and the Boys, going through the gate to the Highway with their suitcase in their hands — away again, who knew where. There was just no future in a little town like you for young people young and ready, they said. But the old ones sat right there with you, Charity, holding your dying hand, rocking and wailing and listening or counting their secret futile beads of hope.

V

YET what were the ways and roads that led me back, I whose ancestors were wheel and well and cellar and loft?

Day after day, night after night a ship plowed and plunged through the water — and we two were on its bow, standing together looking together ahead: now I hear Christy's voice speaking into mine and telling, the way he told me long ago in the woods, in his way, of his life that became mine (now I see it), of the roads he followed away, and of the ways back home (*"Blues" he called me instead of Christy because he said I was so sad. I had left home in you Charity, with Clatzco Skiles, for the Merchant Marines, we had signed up at the Postoffice, and gone away through Texis lyin in cotton, for it was pickin time, and the pickers, draggin their long limp bags behind em across the fields, were like a pack of crawlin wounded animals with broken backs. I passed through Tennysee with niggers' laughter over Memphis, niggers on the steps of*

houses in the September heat; crossed over the catfish rivers.
A fall wind was already blowin in Ohio. I spit in the Beau-
tiful Ohio for luck and good-bye. In New York I took my ship
bound for Panymaw that I had seen like a red appendix on
the map, but they putt Clatzco on a freighter goin I don't
know where. In the ship I was lonesome and afraid, but I did
my work. At night I'd lay in my bunk and think of everthing.
And then I saw a face, fair in its youngman's bearded beauty,
and so much like Follie that I almost cried out "Follie!" I
watched this face while I worked and it swam before me in
my nights in my bunk. I wanted to putt my hand on this hand
and hold it still under mine, made still by his made still. Oh
he was bright and I was dark and I gave him all my darkness
on that ship; but we joined, for all good things in the world,
and to find somethin together; and loved, I never knew I
could do it and was afraid; and on the bow of the ship that
night that he said, "What have we done Christy?"

I said, wonderin too, "But somethin good will come of
this, I know somethin good will come of this . . . "

Only sorrow came).

Day after day, night after night, our ship plowed
through the water filled with flying fishes and dolphins
and the nights so blue and white, the spray flying up like
feathers of white birds, and white birds following us.
Some nights the water was so smooth, so quiet, and we
were so quiet upon it, that the ship glided like a phantom skater; and the moonlight would lie in the wide
gleaming swath following as though the ship turned up,

like a plow, moonlight. Life was in a stunning balance, timeless and directionless, and identities and names were lost. And then some watercurse fell upon us and our names were broken by the brute prow of the ship, like the waves that were broken, and we were anonymous as broken pieces that never can be mended to their whole again. This craft called Ship, this monstrous artifact of builders, held us, broken pieces, within it, trying to find ourselves in each other.

But when the disenchantment came and the voyage ended and the others turned their backs upon the enchantment as though it had been only joke played upon them, or dream, or charade, we, nameless pieces, pieced ourselves together into each other and went away, off the ship, into a world of magic and witchcraft whirling in the twilight glimmer of hope and hopelessness. Who were we and where had we ever come from, what had made us what we were? Charity and the house and all the people in it had been blown away, it seemed, by my breath.

Looking, as we went, toward the water that held beyond us the ship it had spawned, phantom water-egg that had borne us, we stopped; we heard the fogbell forlornly clanging. It had a broken sound that seemed to tell us dread, terror, loss, but some destiny. Waterborn, Glaucus and magician grass, we felt land alien.

At night, in the cities, as we went, the wind was flogging a ragged cloud like an old woman beating a rug,

and the dust fell over the cities. The moon would hang
fat in the East. And looking upon it, we wished we could
find one word, one strong word, small but hard as a
stone, that would mean our aloneness in the world, and
say it in great crying voice, hurling toward the moon.
On the lighted boulevards there was marching pomp
and ceremony and the rattle of laughter, revel and
carousal and a running. There was no name for anyone
or anything. The lonely were waiting on the corners and
in most every park for someone to come — and they
could bruise themselves against each other into at least a
momentary reality upon a bed of peace. (But if I were to
speak of the loneliness *within* love, would anyone understand?)

In the cities certainty was deranged and a crack and
a break were in the once clear voice, a flaw in every
finely woven garment. Some daemon purpose was sown
all in the land. (The only caress that of an image, that of a
coldhanded beauty, like a marble caress. O granite
caress. O granite kiss.)

And in the desert, where we were, the bare scalp of
earth stretched scabrous and feverish under the metallic
light, and the wind would run its lion-toothed comb
through the loose sand and sage, rend them like loose
hair and scale and fling and scatter them over roof and
against us going bitten and stung under the hard tile
sky. Hordes of grasshoppers would ride in on the wind
and shuttle together, clacking their desiccate wings.

There was a steaming vapor out over the tortured desert and the light went hard and percussive so that it might ring like a copper bell if it could be struck, and the world lay brittle as bone. We felt all of bone and rock and metal, we could no longer melt together but stood apart hard as bone and rock. What ruined us? We yearned for water.

Then, in a little town by water, at the Equinox, we broke ourselves against each other, broke forever, broken O broken forever.

O the cry over the waters, what was crying over the waters, what was running all through the waters, ringing the buoys over all the waters? Shadows on the shore, what shadow-people, worn faces like stone metopes, shadow family, shadow kin, hovering together along the shore, near me, always near me.

Walking walking walking round in one's loneliness, up and down in a town. It is cold and the wind blows; the streets are dirty. Because of much rain the trees are green-slimed; the slime is bright and frozen in the streetlights. Yet the beast will not come into the fold. The ultimate agony of aloneness is not to be real; and, unreal, to demoralize love.

The grinding of my feet over ice on the city pavements was over everything frozen, yet when I walked on the pavements something in some others I passed turned a little and bowed to something in me turning; and we greeted each other secretly by a secret turning — but passed on. Yet when I looked in a showwindow I saw my terrible white face, lined and drawn like a dead man's . . . Who would turn to a dead man? *Savior, Savior, hear my humble cry; while on others thou art calling, do no pass me by!* (I would set in the bus stations wantin to talk to somebody, but couldn't, wouldn't . . . I would set and, hearin the wheels of the busses crushin the ice on the pavements, goin off to home for people in them, remember the snow and sleet in the bottomlands and the feet of the birds on the ice-bound bottomlands. And think of in Loosiana when we went there, Mama and Malley and Lauralee and me, when Papa was workin for the rayroad and travelin out of headquarters in Shrevesport; and how we hobbled along like cripples over the first snow in our lives, and fell down on the hard ice, alone in Shrevesport, and cryin, and homesick. And how the only thing we knew to do on Sundays was to ride the streetcar to the end a the line and back for a nickel. In school there I had my first music and all the songs we sang were sad: "My Bonnie Lies over the Ocean" . . .) and think that some of us are preparations for others: that we prepare others for their life — and that that ought to be enough. But the wound is left. How we work on each other like chemicals, like acids and salts and sulphurs; how like lacquer we change surfaces . . . Everything, then, working with and upon everything — with accompanying resistance and damage and error but turning out something changed, finished, prepared to receive something more, to take in and take on something more: pain, wisdom, love. This great, mysterious chemistry going on — praise it.

When the betrayal comes, in the season of disenchantment, my agony goes formless and flies through the world, is only *felt* like wind and cannot be caught into any images or shaped into any meaning, but hovers insubstantial and untouchable; only breathes and whispers and murmurs round me and lulls me into a spell-like dream. *What muss I do?* Then I feel I may never hold or shape a hope again. I forget everything — and I am demoralized and abuse those who love me and go from street to street, betrayed, wandering, drenched in rain. Who am I, bruised so unreal? — what will realize me? — I whirl round and bobble or stand like a statue thrown into the stickerburrs. And then I hear the voices ("Come home, the light's on, come on home, Ben Berryben . . . ") ("Swimma-a-a-a! Swimma-a-a-a! come in 'fore dark . . . ") ("Rescue the Perishing . . . ") ("Boy, Boy come out to the woodshed, I've got somethin to show you, by gum . . . ") ("Draw me, draw me, I will follow") and I melt down like the gingerbread man that ran and ran and ran and melted as he ran. Then I name over and over in my memory every beautiful and loved image and idea I have ever had, and praise them over and over, saying, Granny Ganchion, I touch you and name you; Folner, I touch you and name you; Aunty, Malley, Swimma, Christy, I touch you and name you and claim you all. It is like a procession through the rooms of this house, saying, now this is the hall and there is the bottled ship and the seashell, this is the breezeway, there is the well, here is the map in the kitchen and here is the watery mirror in which, behold, is my face, *me*, my face . . .

That people could come into the world in a place they could not at first even name and had never known before; and that out of a nameless and unknown place they could grow and move around in it until its name they knew and called with love, and call it HOME, and put roots there and love others there; so that whenever they left this place they would sing homesick songs about it and write poems of yearning for it, like a lover; remembering the grouping of old trees, the fall of slopes and hills, the lay of fields and the running of rivers; of animals there, and of objects lived with; of faces, and names, all of love and belonging, and forever be returning to it or leaving it again!

Out of this suffering a vision of violence: of striking beaks of horn; of blood upon my thigh; of fallen and falling birds. Fallen wings of leaves (what silent terrible flock rows over across the heavens, dropping lost wings, blood-green and yellow, lined like the palms of phantom hands, upon us?) drift down upon us.

So it all ends, in wordlessness, and in my tears.

Yet something forms within the world of a tear, shaped by the world that caused it; something takes shape within this uttered breath that builds an image of breath:

VI

BEHOLD the house . . .

Now ruin has passed over all that fallen splendid house and done ruin's work on it. Now, ruin (of childhood) returning to ruin, come, purged of that bile and gall of childhood, come through the meadow called Bailey's Pasture that is spun over with luminous dandelions like a million gathered shining heads, through random blooming mustard and clover and bitterweeds, over the grown-over path that was a short-cut to town when there was no circus or revival tent there. Pass one brown spotted cow folded there (remember her name as a calf was Roma and a good ride) and munching the indestructible bitterweed cud of time, and pass around the silent laboring, nervous civilization of an anthill that swarms and traffics on and on beyond the decline of splendid houses or the fall of broken cisternwheels. The slow grinding of cud, even and

measured, the twinkling, red, timeless quarry of ants
and the eternal, unalterable cycle of flowers — first the
white, then the pink, then red to blue to purple and
finally to sunflower yellow — round and round, turning
and turning, moving and moving: they mock the crooked mile that families walk, suffering and failing and
passing away, over their crooked stile, into a crooked
Beulah Land.

If you come this way about this time of a time,
through Bailey's Pasture, you will then come to and have
to cross over the warped, rusted railroad tracks of the
MKT, called Katy Railroad; and, having crossed the
rails, you will behold before you this house. You think
you hear a voice — from the shuttered window? From
the front gallery? From the cellar, the loft? — murmuring, "But who comes here, across the pasture of bitterweeds, wading in through the shallows, home?"

If you be Berryben Ganchion you have returned after a long long time and too late. For your mother, Malley
Ganchion, has gone blind from cataracts that kept her
half-blind for such a long time, sitting by the closed
shutter in this house, alone, waiting for you to come
back.

If you be Sue Emma Starnes, you are too late, too;
and if you be any other, then you have returned for all of
them, for all their sakes, come to rummage and explore,
in your hour, and find a meaning, and a language and a
name.

Open the rusted iron gate and step across the stickerburrs blooming in the grass, go round past the rotted tire where the speckled canna used to live and turn towards the cisternwheel that does not turn. See the cistern, rusted and hollow and no water in it, and the wheel of the windmill wrecked and fallen and rats playing over the ruin. The wheel is like an enormous metal flower blighted by rust. Bend down to touch the fallen petals and, bending, hear the grinding groan of the wheel that begins to turn again in your brain of childhood, rasping the overtone of loneliness and moaning the undertone of wonder. Remember how it rose up on long legs out of the round, deep, lidded stock tub, and remember once when the lid was left off how the child of a Negro washwoman (recall her poking, head wrapped in a scrap of red bandanna, the steaming black iron pot full of Starnes and Ganchion clothes) climbed up and fell into the tub and was drowned and how the cows come to drink bellowed to find its corpse.

Now the wheel lies in a grotesque ruin by the rusted and empty tub, and weed grows up between its metal petals (and sunflowers, crooking over after the sun, mock because they turn) and rats scuttle over the wreckage. It lies like the emblazonment of a fallen house, blazoned by rat's scratches and rust engravings, the intaglios carved in by decay; and, vanquished and defiled like the coat of arms of Starnes and Ganchion, it lies unturned by the wind that brushes against it but cannot turn it, useless and disempowered. (Once its turning was like a silver burning in the autumn sunlight, flashing and turning in its gyre so that wind in it meant water and families lived by wind, as a sailed ship. And if the wind came from the direction of the sawmill it bore and scattered over the house the piney pollen of sawdust, and if from the direction of the river bottomlands, the scents of pines glistening far from the hot inferno of kilns, and the sweet breath of the Charity Riverwoods.

Often I stood, boy blown in the wind that blew upon the cisternwheel and turned it, in an autumn dusk, a big hand holding mine, and watched the whirling of the wheel. I felt myself a steady fixed point on the earth round which a whirling gathered and spun as a center. Then it was that I seemed to be no one, to belong to no one (he holding my hand) and suddenly beholding the russet light of the turning sumach tree in the pasture (pulled down and stolen from all light by that terrible winter's long ropes of solid ice), I thought, *O I am leaf and I am wind and I am light. Something in the world links faces and leaves and rivers and woods and wind together and makes of them a string of medallions with all our faces on them, worn forever round our necks, kin.*

Dare you go into the house? Go, entering through the back door (out of which you used to throw the water from the washstand to the chickens gathered waiting for it. Oh the mournful mewling of Aunty's young broilers waiting at the steps for you in the mornings or at dusks when you would wash at the washstand: they haunt you, the calls of the broilers, their plaints and plaintive whines in the yard) which opens on the screened-in breezeway. There seems some hand, big and broken-knuckled, waiting at the door taking your hand to lead you.

On this breezeway in the summer afternoons she held the flyswatter like a scepter and Uncle Jimbob sat, poorly and silent, on a little barrel, and all of them, the Cousins and Aunts and Uncles and other kin, just sitting there with nothing to do, nowhere to go, nothing to dress up for, just sitting. And then, hearing wheels on the road and running to the kitchen window, she shouted "The gypsies!", and all of them gathered at the windows, watching the bright gypsies jingle down the road, bright and quick and going someplace, and none of them saying a word, all of them gathered at the windows, looking through the windows.

Her drinking well was right in the house at the end of the long back porch next to the indoor privy (there was a crooked one outside beyond the chickens, but in it were hornets). This was the only magic thing, the dark, enchanted well that held the beautiful voice prisoner, down below the shimmering water. When you cried down, "Hello! hello!", it answered back only, "O! . . . O!", in a wailing young girl's voice.

When Uncle Jimbob had to clean the well he would

draw out all the water and lower you down into the
darkness on a little wooden sling of a seat. You dreamt of
it, and often — forever — (for you had been so bred as a
well-creature, brother to the bucket, lowered empty and
pulled up full and brimming clear to be drunk down by
waiting thirst — child of wheel and cistern-child, with
gift of turning) felt the terrible descent of alienation from
face and voice and light into empty, lightless loneliness
(but O Granny Ganchion, joined to you, below); and
knew, that once you were pulled up (by whom, what
hand?) into light and warmth again, you would somewhere in you be changed by the well-terror and commit-
ted to make it known to those on the summer breezeway
as vision, for all their sakes. For each time you ascended
— by hard will, by choice, by courage, you had a
responsibility to the vision of descent. Down on the cold
sand floor of the well you crouched, cold and trembling,
and heard the mysterious voices beyond the well (as you
heard them from your pallet often, whispering in the
next room) talking in an easy summer afternoon:
Aunty's and Malley's and Granny's and Swimma's and
the others', and wondered, alien there, if you would
ever be joined to them again — or if you were, whether
you could ever really tell them what your terror in the
well had been; or heard the voices round the blue hole
far above, voices of the gathered faces round the rim
calling down "Boy! Boy! Can you hear your name?"

　　(The wheel is broken at the cistern, the rope at the

well is raveled and rotten, the bucket is rusted and leaky; and there is never a hand on the windlass now.)

And in the front yard in the late summer afternoons when the children played barefoot upon the sticker-burrs, all her kin sat rocking round her on the porch and she spat snuff into the front yard and rocked and said, "This is an old house. That was pore Mama and Papa's room there. I remember pore Mama and Papa sleeping in that front room where Malley and Walter Warren and Jessy and Berryben live now when all of us was children."

And the children in the front yard running bare-footed over the stickerburrs, singing "Go in and out the windows, go in and out the windows, go in and out the windows, for we have gained this day."

Or, in the game of Statue, all the Starnes and Ganchion young thrown into frozen poses, bent-over mourning shapes or vain or heroic arabesques — so that in memory they seem like a pavilion of ruined statuaries. (Folner even then would cheat a pose into some careless, blase stance, but he could not ransom his face.)

The little train would go by in front of the house and stop all rocking and any game and where, where was it going? And who was the wild-faced man in the dirty cap who waved the gloved-black hand from the engine as it passed? And what was he trying to say to all of them, to the children playing games in the big front yard round

the speckled canna and the big ones rocking on the long
gallery in the swing and wicker rockers? Here they sat
and ran as he passed, and oh who *was* he, this leering,
magical, terrible man who waved the great gloved-black
hand at them from the little engine as it passed, going
where? coming from where? Oh they said it was going to
Riverside, but that train was going *everywhere.*

"And oh," Aunty said, "we ain't got a chanct, we
ain't got a chanct in this world. Jimbob's down in the
back and got hemorrhoids and a stone in his bladder and
cain't carpenter or work at the roundhouse or even lift a
good size squash; and the garden's dry and burnin up in
the burnin sun and we cain't buy feed for the cows and
chickens and I don't know what we'll ever do, just set
here on this porch and rock and spit until we die one day
and be buried by our pore relations. And Swimma fin-
ishin high school next year and then where does she go
and what does she do? If she goes wild like that
Willadean Clegg I'd rather see her dead, I declare to you
all and to the good Lord I'd rather see her dead. But I can
see it comin. Ought to have her a business course in
Palestine, but who on earth can afford to pay for the kind
of course she needs at Miz Cratty's Select Business
College in Palestine? And Maidie marryin Fred that runs
a streetcar in Dallas and who can live off the money they
pay you to run a streetcar in Dallas? And Malley and
Walter Warren unhappy and little Jessy sickly — and
this infernal little town of Charity dead and rottin away

with only the Ralph Sandersons havin the money and all the rest of us pore as nigras and our teeth bad and my side hurtin day and night with the change a life and no money to see a specialist in Dallas (Jimbob, Jimbob, the pigs is in the peapatch again, but don't run. Walk, Jimbob, mind your back). My Lord, guess we'll all die in a pile right here, with the pigs in the peapatch and nobody carin, nobody carin.

"Why? On New Year's Day I cook my cabbage and make my pillow slips."

"Aunty, why does the Widow Barnes just sit on her porch?"

Oh all the porches in the little town had them rocking on them, sitting, sitting; and the crops burning up under the burning sun and the teeth going bad and stones in the bladders and the town rotting away and no place to go, no place to go.

The Ku Klux Klan went riding riding. You saw the fiery cross on Rob Hill in the summer nighttime and you knew some poor crazy riverbottom Negro was goin to burn, was going to run shrieking down Main Street in tar and feathers.

"Aunty, Aunty, what is that noise by the woodstove?"

"Be still, Boy. It's only the rats in your Aunty's woodbox."

"Oh the sad sad days when all of us was young," she said, and spat and rocked. "You know when Mama

passed on, she left me all her old crockery. There was
some big pitchers with roses handpainted on them. And
then the old Nigra Mary Bird who cleaned for Mama for
years just took them all, saying they was rightfully hers
because she was the only one that ever was kind to
Mama and rightfully deserved them. Everthing we ever
had is gone. What they don't steal away from us we lose
by drout or a plague or a rottin away. Life is hard and
only sufferin and it does no good to any of us and how
we ever bear it I don't know. But we have it to do and
we've got to be strong about it and try not to be blue
about it and go on in trial and tribylation. But how life
changes and the things that happen to us in this world
are like stories to be read and I declare the great God
don't even know sometimes the dreadful things that
happen to us; and oh Boy, Boy, let me push back the hair
from your eye. Goin to be wrinkled as old man Nay
down by the sawmill, worst suit a hair I ever saw. Come
to me — lemme roach back ya hair. The Ganchions are
the blight of Charity, and I know it, worse than boll weevils, worse than a pest a hoppers, the Devil incarnit,
despise the day we all come here from Sour Lake, us
rawsin bellies; Charity ruined us. Don't frown so, Boy,
don't worry so; commere, lemme roach back the hair
from ya eye . . . "

"Aunty, Aunty, who am I? Who are we? What kin
are we all to each other?"

"The gingerbread man he ran and ran; and melted

as he ran. On the nose of the fox he melted down into the tears of the fox that ran . . . When we was all in Sowlake with Mama and Papa, runnin in the fields and playin in the wagon it seemed like nothin ever could happen to any of us. (Papa played a jew's-harp on the screenporch in the evenins.) When Walter Warren married Malley we all nearly died, I tell you, nearly killed us. That was the beginnin of the whole trouble; then we come to Charity, then the Starnes come into this house, one by one, right in on us, till we'uz all here together. Ever year got harder and harder, drouts come and floods come and children come; the whole world was changing, preachers said the end a the world was comin, wickedness everwhere and sickness everwhere, and no money.

"Maidie was so sweet and quiet, always minded me and never give me on lick a trouble. When the Revival meetin was acrost in Bailey's Pasture we'd go and there sang the best quartet I ever heard in my life, the Sunshine Boys; and Fred Suggs was in it, a tenor with a beautiful solo voice. When the Sunshine Boys sang, *Man of the world, why stand ye idle all the day? Look up to Christ, he will forgive, your sins he'll wash away! Then be prepared to meet thy God and of the feast partake; The King of Kings is ruler there, he guards the golden gate!* this was just about the peacefulest thing in the world; and when Fred Suggs would chime in with his beautiful tenor voice: *Is there anyone here who is not prepared to pass through the golden gate? Be ready, for soon the time*

*will come to enter the golden gate. Don't let it be said, too
late, too late, to enter the golden gate. Be ready, for soon the
time will come, to enter the golden gate.*

"Well, Fred Suggs was just the finest boy, we
brought him across the tracks to Sunday dinner and he
and Maidie picked a watermelon from the patch and we
had it and then they went walkin down the tracks afterwards. I knew they wanted to marry and in the Fall Fred
Suggs come back to Charity and they married and went
away to Dallas. It nearly killed me to pack her suitcase,
but I waved at them from the gate and they went on off to
Dallas. Pore Maidie, she cries ever night for Charity and
all of us in this house, and I wish she would come back,
the city's no place for Maidie, no place for pore pineywoods folks, Maidie's no city girl, never was farther
than White Rock Bridge on Fourth of July picnics before
she went to Dallas. She don't even know her neighbors,
they work all day, and on Sunday she takes the children
to Sunday School and then they ride the streetcar to the
end a the line and back. Sometimes she goes to town to
Kress a little, but that's about all. The time they made me
come to Dallas to see the dentist was awful, firewagons
howlin their sireens ever minute, those streetcars grindin day and night, just couldn't stand it. 'This town's
burnin down and they're all killin each other, I cain't
sleep or set still and I'm goin back home,' I said; and
declared I uz comin back to Charity. Said I'd order my
teeth from Sears (certainly wouldn't have Doctor Stokes

in Charity to make my teeth, that drunkard; he's ruined ever mouth in Charity).

"But pore little Maidie in that duplex in that city; I wish she'd come back here. Wish all of em would come on back here and we could have our reunions that we used to have when all the Starnes ud come in from the woods. Never saw so much squash and yella-legged chicken in your life, all the young Starnes not a one under six feet, and the pretty, timid girls — where have they all gone? I tell you the Devil walked in the river-bottoms — and cussed this town.

"I just want to set right here in this house, don't want to see nobody, don't care if they all never come here again, just want to set here in this old rotten house until I die. Never had nothin, never will have nothin, none of us ever had a chanct and I don't care any more, be glad when I die, wish I'd hurry up, then it'll be all over with."

Oh you ain't got a chanct, you ain't got a chanct in this world. You are down in the back and got hemorrhoids and a stone in your bladder and you can't carpenter or work at the roundhouse and the garden's dry and burnin up in the burnin sun and you can't buy feed for the cows and chickens and I don't know what you'll ever do, just sit there on the porch and rock and spit and die one day and be buried by your poor relations. And the infernal little town dead and rottin away and all of you poor as niggers and your teeth bad and your sides hurtin day and night and no money to see a doctor in Dallas.

"(And Jimbob, Jimbob, the pigs is in the peapatch but don't run, walk, Jimbob. Mind your back, Jimbob. My Lord guess we'll all die in a pile right here with the pigs in the peapatch and nobody carin.)"

Nobody carin.

Now a spider lives unbothered in the doormat that never knows a pawing foot upon it.

There is the kitchen gathered around the great worn woodstove. A faded map is still tacked on the wall. You hear the mice kicking in the turned-over oatmeal. And you hear the wind that lopes like a spectral rider round and round the house, whirls down the flues and chutes into the woodstove and thrashes the ashes and blows a wild little horn in the hollows of the stove. Then you hear a melody from a farther room and it is the wind blowing a tune in the closed shutter in the room where Malley Ganchion lived on like a mouse in the house after all the others had gone, hoping some redemption for them all would come.

Some appetite waits and lurks in the world, you remark; it is some great hunger, insect and rodent and decay hunger. This seems suddenly to be a law of the universe. Insect, mold, rat, rust, death — all wait for and get the human plunder in the end, to carry the carrion away. The vultures of this greed hover and plane over us all our lives, waiting to drop down. The leaf has its caterpillar, the stalk mildew and the worm lies crooked in the bud. And observe the little white lice, dandruff in the golden head of the marigold, the gall chancres and fistulas on the rosebush. See the shale of fly carcasses in the spiderwebs, of caught hornets and flying ants, wings folded like a closed fan (the dead of this house lie fastened in what web, stretched over what blue Kingdom?), bits of wings and antennae, all debris. The dirt-dobbers' knobs of mud, lathed round and whorled smooth, hang like many lightless lanterns — because there is no hand to knock them down. The insects have taken over — we fight them back all our lives, but in the end they come victoriously in, our inheritors. Look in the corners, under things — find the little purewhite puffs and tents in which some whiskery thing lives, find the thousandlegs and stinkbugs and doodlebugs and Junebugs, find fantastic bugs with shielded backs and delicate marks and brilliant colors and designs. See a caught mouse in a trap — set by what futile, mocked hand? — rotted to a frail skull and a vertebra. And see over the boards of the faded floor the Sienese lines of tracks and roads and tunnels and cross-hatched marks and trails. In the bins and cannisters are weevils; the roaches, unmolested, are grown big. The legged armies have come into this house. This is the slow eating away — mold and canker and mildew and must, gall and parasite, lice and little speckled ticks and grooved worms. In a corner of the pantry (where you often ran to

hide from old Mr. Hare, passing in his rumbling wagon
calling "paa-ahs! paa-ahs!") discover a ruined still life of
left vegetables, whiskered and leprosied, and rotted
fruit spotted with pustules and the stippled fuzz of
fungus. (You remember the glassy picture in the dining
room, where you ate on Sundays, that was of a sad dead
blue duck dangling down a golden-flecked and purple-
speckled head — with staring eyes that watched you eat
— and pears and peaches round him; and feel that picture's ruin before you.)

And all so quiet is this eating away, except for the
wind that winds a mummy cloth around the fallen
splendid house delivered to its inheritors.

So this is why when often as you came home to it,
down the road in a mist of rain, it seemed as if the house
were founded on the most fragile web of breath and you
had blown it. Then you thought it might not exist at all
as built by carpenters' hands, nor had ever; and that it
was only an idea of breath breathed out by you who,
with that same breath that had blown it, could blow it all
away.

VII

LED BY THIS HAND you go to the well, made of stone and minaretted by a slender windlass where the rusty and battered bucket hangs like a ruined bell on a rotted and raveled rope in its tower. If I should cry down some name in this well, you think, what voice would rouse and speak out of this well to me? You cry down the name of Sue Emma Starnes, calling "Swimma-a-a! Swimma-a-a-a!" (come in 'fore dark) and you hear the round wavering answer, like a voice heard under water, "And all the daughters of musick shall be brought low . . . "

And then the long story, told out like a speaking mouth filled with wind, opening and closing in the wind:

"Well, when Swimma finished Charity High," the well-voice says, "she stayed around home for awhile but then got restless and packed her suitcase and went to

Dallas to stay with Maidie, her sister, you know. Right away that girl blossomed out in Dallas, it was just her style.

"Got her a job in J.C. Pennys sellin paints and hatchets and hardware things, but soon they learned that Swimma Starnes didn't belong back with the hardware. She had talent at fixin and arrangin and when they saw that she was right smart at decoratin they put her in the windows, gave her the job of sprucin up the showwindows. Naturally Swimma loved to be in a showwindow, don't you just *know?* It was the Ganchion in her.

"Then because she had a real cute shape, built like a carnival kewpie doll, she got this job modelin at Neiman Marcuses. This really changed Swimma, let me tell *you.* Got to smokin cigarettes through a cigarette holder long as a beanshooter, would wear her black hair (she's part Indian, you know) piled up on her head one day like a African and flowin all down her back the next like a huzzy. She moved right out of her sister Maidie's duplex into a suite at the Stoneleigh Manor, said Maidie was an old fogy and ought to move back to the sticks, meanin Charity, and made fun of the Sunshine Boys that practiced ever Wednesday night at the duplex.

" 'You oughta go back home and hep Mama and Papa,' Maidie said to her, and this made Swimma so mad she had one of her tantrums, shoutin, *'I'm* not goin back there, it's a cinch. Why should *I* go back there, that's where *you* belong. *I'm* not goin to wash over a rickety ole washstand covered with oilcloth and ruin my complexion with lava soap and go out through the cold and rain to the privy when I can have Princess Pat Preparations and a pink ruffled boudoir in a suite all my own *with adjoinin bath* at the Stoneleigh.'

"Now just a word of well-wisdom here. You remember Ola Peabody's neck — how it was scaly like the bark of a tree? The end of all beauty and swank is Ola's neck, scaly and crusted and crinkled. Josh left Ola for a twenty-two-year-old girl. His marriage to Ola was as if he had abused her and deformed her for twenty-seven years and then throwed her on a trash pile. Look what marriage does to a woman. Look what it did to poor Ola — a big tumor is all she has; and gray dry hair and a scaly neck. No childrun, she could never have any. While Josh has kept himself up good, with still good teeth, never went to a dentist in his life (except once when he thought he had pyorrheah and we nearly had to bury him because he thought all his front teeth would turn black — and I wish they had) — and a figure so straight and no pot like middle-aged men have and not even bald. He found this girl Eula Pearl and is startin his youth all over again with her. These nasty men. Men are so nasty, hair all over 'em — did you ever see a man that wouldn't scratch where it itched, I don't care *where* it is? Nasty things, that's all they think of. 'I want youth and beauty,' Josh said. Why of course, so do all of us want

youth and beauty, but how can Ola have youth and
beauty after being bounced around, used like a dray-
horse, after liftin and scrubbin and servin him like a ser-
vant? Josh is a big Shrine, wears that tassled cap often as
he can, laughin and struttin and bitin a cigar. I wonder if
those Shrines know what he's done in his personal life?
Ola ought to write them a good letter about him and tell
them all what he has done. That's what Miz Shively did.
When she found out what was goin on between Brother
Shively, preacher of the First Baptist Church, and Mrs.
Branch, a widow, she just called a meetin of the Board on
Tuesday evenin and read before them a letter about
what she had found out. That was the end of Brother
Shively, he was transferred to Beaumont.

   "But the point is that the end of all beauty is Ola's
neck, scaly and crusted and crinkled like a work-glove.

   "Well, anyway, at a personality contest of some
kind Swimma won it and was sent to New York in a air-
plane to walk up and down in some long silk dress ithout
any bosom to it, jes straps, mind you, and nekkid as a jay
half-way down to her waist. She was judged a beauty
everwhere and they was a flyin her all over the country
like some prize heifer to show off, even to Hawaya and
everplace.

   "Then she went on the stage (just like Folner
Ganchion, everbody could all see it) — that little country
girl Swimma Starnes that everbody knew in Charity
Texis — and made a mint a money I guess and became a

real celebrity, you couldn't turn through the magazines
ithout comin upon Swimma Starnes smokin a cigarette
or cocked up on a wall like Humpty Dumpty with her
long legs bare in a bathin suit no wider than a hair
ribbon. Naturally she attracted the men like flies —
that's what she *wanted*. Like her old grandma, had to
have whiskers round her, had to have a pair of pants
round her noon and night. Had more men friends than
you could shake a stick at, got expensive presents flung
at her from all of them, I *know* on account of I was told.

"She jes disinherited all her family. While she was
prancin round half-nekkid in some personality show,
her pore mother Lauralee Starnes was a brushin down
dirtdobbers' nests from a outhouse in Charity Texis
with a hickrystick, or spittin snuff in a tincan on the
front gallry.

"Then Lauralee and Jimbob Starnes got word, jes
on a postcard from Miami, Florida, that Swimma had
married, had married some rich man (we think he was a
Jew) with some business, nobody knew what. And
Swimma started havin the little babies with big heads.
First one was a boy with a head big as a watermelon and
shaped like one. That little freak lived and lived, head
kept gettin bigger and bigger, and they would come and
measure it and measure it, but it wouldn't die, really got
strong and healthy as an ox, and jes lay there in its bed,
huge and strong and an idiot, thrashin like a whale and
slobberin all over the bedclothes. The wicked have their

hell right here on earth, I said. Well, that thing lived to
be *nine* years ole and no doctor in the country could do a
thing for it; until one mornin they found it dead in its
bed and that uz a blessin.

"Now Swimma will really come to her senses, we
all thought; it's taken such a tragedy to shake some sense
into her head. She grieved and grieved over that little
monster, had a nervous breakdown and took to heavy
drinkin, and we all waited for her to come home. We
thought she would divorce that rich man that people
said was some big Miami gambler. But nope, she stayed
on with him and what do you think? She had *another*
bigheaded freak. Another boy. But it lived only a year.
You know ther've been a lot of freaks in Charity, that
Lindalou Bell had a bigheaded baby like that and they
said it uz because Simp Bell had lived round among the
nigras out at Grapeland when he uz buildin the Highway through there. Oh there was a row over that —
Lindalou's family, the Bensons (been in Charity for
years and years) blamed it on Simp's old daddy, Dr. Bell,
a perpetual drunkard and had insanity somewhere in iz
famly; and Simp's famly said twuz Lindalou's fault, that
she was diseased and oh I don't know what all, it was all
terrible and one of the worse scandals of Charity, the
two famlies literally fightin in the street and the whole
town talkin — you know how a town talks. Then there
was that little deformity that the Barkers had, turned out
to be real talented, went away with a carnival as a

frogboy last we heard; and the Saxton boy, blown big as a balloon, couldn't walk with him on the sidewalk, he was so stout; and those little deaf-and-dumb children of the Royces, flashin finger language, it was so sad to see them. And there're a lot of other Charity freaks, too, in my estimation (but they'll all come home; like the cows they'll all come home) — Smollett Thompson (let's not mention *him*) and the rest — leave them alone and they'll all come home, late or soon. What got into this house? What got into this town? Houses and towns hold their tragedies and could tell some things if they could speak. You know how Christy Ganchion left with the Skiles boy for the Merchant Marines. Somethin happened to Christy, somewhere, that nobody'll ever know. Christy's quiet as a tomb — and dumb as a doornail, some said (but *I* don't believe it — still water runs deep), like Thrash Clegg, they say, but you cain't make me believe it. Anyway when he come back they had a time with him for awhile. Then you know how he married Otey Bell from up in the woods beyond the mill and what all happened, but that's another story, don't ask me.

"But anyway — one at a time, I'm speakin of Swimma Starnes, now — after this second freak of Swimma's died she jes went straight to the dogs, they say. She got to be jes common trash. Her rich husband divorced her, *then*, after he had ruint her, but still she wouldn't come home.

"Well, and then we heard that she had gone to New

Orleens and played around and drunk around and married a little ole jockey. Seen his picture once and he's as drawn up and spiney as Ole Man Nay and looks a hundred years old, bout as big as a banty, but they have to be that little, they say, so as to be light on a racin horse. He had a lotta money, too. Swimma had always said that she was goin to find a man with lots a money and get out of this town. She sure did, too.

"And then they discovered oil over round Conroe, the Miracle City. Ole Jimbob Starnes' father had owned some land around there, and who should pop up in Charity one bright day but Miss Swimma Starnes, grinnin out of furs that haltered her like a horsecollar and practically dragged the ground, and on her head a whole bluebird for a hat, tail (as long as you know what) and all. Her wicked life had clawed deep lines all over her face as though she had been fightin wilecats and her eyes were swollen and sick lookin. Because of arthritis (from liquor poisonin, we heard) she dragged one leg a little, but you couldn't hardly notice it if you didn't look for it. She smelled oil, that Swimma, all the way over in New Orleens she smelled it. She was all sugar and cream, bringin as a present a seashell that had written on it PLAYGROUND OF THE WORLD — thas all she brought, ceptin herself; and pore ole Lauralee, sick, sweepin the floors before her — until Swimma found out that the Starnes hadn't paid taxes on that land for years — now how *could* they? *we* knew that — and *then* you shoulda heard the Princess Swimma.

" 'You ole fogies here in Charity don't know what the world's like beyond the riverbottoms, sit here and shrivel up and blow away in the wind; and when you get a chance to make a little money and rise above all this and get some security and a little ease you let it slip through your fingers like sawdust, letting everything rot and go to pot and seed, I'm ashamed of all of you, haven't got any more sense than a stick of stovewood, you make me tarred.'

"All of this in some accent, New York or Loosiana or Florida accent, I don't know, I cain't do it right, but not like Charity talks. Oh she was a devil.

"Well, she went back to New Orleens — that little ole banty come drivin up for her in a black sedan of some kind longer'n the Katy Locomotive and they went off ballin the jack in a cloud of black Charity dust. Pore ole Lauralee.

"Know where she is now? Back in Texis far's Borger, that clost but no farther (that little banty jockey jes flew away, don't know where or why, guess the last racinhorse Swimma saw him on jes kept goin). Runs a boardin house (and a little of everthing *else*) for oilmen, hope she's satisfied, somebody that saw her said she'll hear a dirty joke from any roughneck that comes in and sets down with one to tell, laughin loud and slappin her thigh and talkin about *anything*. Has a diamon ring big as a hensegg and a wart on her nose (and I'm glad) which

she says is a beautyspot . . . Lauralee still said till she
died, pore ole thing, that Swimma'd come back home to
Charity, but she didn't. But this's not all . . .

"When they buried Christy Ganchion, who should
crop up for the funeral but Miss Perfecto. (You know
they had the services in the old house, not in the church,
and the casket was so big (he was a big man) they had to
putt it through the winda under the chinaberry tree.
They putt him in's old room, kept him there for three
days with always a light on; and walkin down the road
past the house you could see through the chinaberry
leaves and through the winda Christy lyin there in iz
box in iz room quiet as ever.) Only the young ones was
left, Starnes and Ganchion — Maidie (she was there
with her two boys, grown men) and Berryben (not there,
still away somewhere) and Swimma. Hattie Clegg come
in from Houston, and drawn with her Bell's Palsy, pore
ole thing, best Christian in this world, what a life she's
had. Swimma seemed the same. Said she was still lookin
for a good man (she'd run through I don't know how
many like a pig eatin acorns). Anyway, turns out that
when Granny died (*finely*, after livin on and on and sayin, 'I'll live to be a hunderd just to hound you all'; they
had her goiter taken out, said twould bring back her
hearin, and some said it did, that that's what killed her,
that towards the last she heard Christy, and that when
she heard the whine of the planeing mill, dyin, she said,
'Listen, what's that? I knew it; wherever I go, above or

below, there'll be a sawmill.' They'd had to lock the
cellardoor after she got so feeble, to keep her from going
down to the rootcellar to find somethin she said was
waitin for her to come and get.) she'd left a little money
in a fruitjar for Christy. There uz only Christy and
Malley left now and Christy left Malley in the house with
the Cleggs next door to look after her (they come over
one day, to borry somethin no doubt, and found Malley
dead in her chair by the opened shutter. Mice had made
nests in the windasill out of the gray hair she'd combed
out as she set there day in and day out, and there uz even
sparrows' nests in the shutters and dirtdobber hives.
Some said she'd opened the shutter to call out to a wagon
that uz passin by; and others that she'd seen somebody
she knew comin acrost Bailey's Pasture — we'll never
know. It's so sad, the life of this house, and seems like
nothing but deaths, but then that's the way anything
ends, finally, ain't it? We all have to die . . .) and went
away to Houston, nobody knew what for but seemed
like he was lookin for somethin. Somebody said they
saw him wanderin in the streets lookin like a dead man,
and passed him by; others said he was sellin newspapers on a corner, and still some more said he'd joined
a Mission. Anyway it turns out that *Swimma was in
Houston too* and that she come to Christy on the street
corner and got money from him often, sayin she uz sick
and broke. *No wonder she come to his funeral,* they had
this between them. I think *this* death nearly killed her,

but you'd never know it, she'd never let on she was hurt by anything, never in her life.

"She jes made a list of all the old dishes after the burial and left. Maidie said she only wanted the churn that Aunty her mother had churned in.

"Somethin wild and cussed in that girl — but somethin else, too; cain't put your finger on it. She'll come to a violent end, you watch. We'll all hear of it one day, just wait'n see. It's jes the saddest thing I ever heard tell of.

"Pore ole Lauralee Starnes . . . "

And then the well-voice dies away and somewhere in the long grownover yard you think you hear Swimma's husky girl's voice, crying as she flung down cousins into statues among the stickerburrs.

VIII

YOU CRY down, "Hattie, Hattie, Hattie Clegg!" and wait; and then you hear a faraway watery voice that rises from deep below to the surface like a bubble, bubbling and warbling, "Ho-o-o-ome — ho-o-o-ome," and breaks and says like a silvery crying: "Anybody home . . . ?" and echoes "Ho-o-o-ome . . . " It is the calling voice of Hattie Clegg who lived in the crumbling house beyond this house and used to come so often to see everybody in this house, always calling at the back door "Anybody home . . . ?" before she went off to Houston to work for the S.P.

"Nobody is at home anymore anywhere in the world . . . " Hattie's voice murmurs; and you want to answer, "Hattie, Hattie, every home in the world is no home for you and me, we are meant to go from home to home and call if they are home (and only strangers break out through some unconsidered door like a bird out of a

clock and chime terror) and leave again, for some other
door."

And then Hattie speaks out of the well to you . . .

"After a bizniss course at Miz Cratty's Select
Bizniss College in Palestine, where I learned Gregg
Shorthand and comtometer and typin, I came to the city,
got this job with the rayroad, been here twenty-five
years.

"O my folks! Never shoulda left Charity, I guess,
but helped em there, ever paycheck I got, sent a tithe of it
home to em, Mama and Papa and Willadean and Gilbert
and Thrash.

"Got Willadean through high school, struggled to
get her finished only to see her marry a widower from up
at Sanderson with three childrun. Somethin in Charity
ruined Willadean, prissed her all up and sent her
straight to ruination. It uz that C.C.C. Camp out at
Groveton did it; made a wicked girl out of Willadean.
Then she worked at the C.O.D. Café, met all the wrong
kind, the sawmill boys and the roughnecks from the oilfields and the just plain tramps of Charity.

"Willadean O Willadean, I nursed you like my very
own when you was little, washed you in winter by the
cookstove, wiped off smut from your little hands twenty
times a day, washed you and fed you and played with
you under the shadetree and swang you in the tire-
swing, shook down pussimons and called doodlebugs
and picked goobers — anything you wanted. Carried

you on my hip round the place, day in and day out, till I
pulled my side loose, made me slouched like I am today.
Can still feel you astride my hip, clingin there like a little
warm possum on to me wherever I went. Sometimes you
was as heavy as a croakersack of roastinears, but I went
on totin you, pullin my very insides out for you.

"Guess I made a mistake in leavin em there in
Charity, but it was up to the boys to help make the livin
and I had this chanct for this job in the city. What in the
world would they have ever done without me? It was always, 'Hattie Hattie kin you come home to Charity this
weekend cause the front porch is fallin in and we got to
get it fixed and Papa is drawn double with rheumatism
and Mama can't squat even to gather eggs from the
henhouse.' Or, 'Hattie Hattie, come home on the bus
soon as you get off on Saturday noon, count of
Willadean's in trouble by a drummer that came through
Charity sellin Watkins Products.'

"Never had a life of my own, always workin and
doin for others, till suddenly I'm an old woman, fifty,
and an old maid, kissed once at the Charity Chatauqua
by the best-lookin man of Charity County but never had
time to follow it up, never had time to give to kissin and
courtin, had to let him go, Huck Chandler uz his name.

"Remember once I went in the C.O.D. Café after
Willadean and what did I see but that young priss stand-
in on her tiptoes on some scales that said upon them,
'Your wate and fate,' and a young roughneck graspin her

round the lower waist and both of them giglin to beat the
band. I could see Willadean's fate right there, didn't
have to putt no penny in no machine to ask *her* fate.
Well, I said to myself, 'Hattie you're a Christian and like
a mother to Willadean, raised her from the cradle,
nursed her and washed her and fed her and toted her
like your very own, it's up to you to get her home and do
some talkin to her.' But I decided to jes set down first
without makin any fuss that might let her know I uz
there and to jes watch this Miss Willadean. The C.O.D.
Café was jes full, people at the machines, all at the coun-
ter, ever seat at the tables was filled with somebody from
the Charity sawmill or the C.C.C. Camp out at Groveton
or the oilfields, smokin and drinkin their beer and bottles of whisky under the tables; and the nickelodeon was
on the rampage, playin at the moment Ding Dong Bells.
Miss Willadean was in her glory, I could see that; prissin
in and out like a priss-ike at the tables, switchin here
and there, laughin and cuttin up with the rowdies and
singin right with the nickelodeon as she waited on
them, 'Ding Dong bells are ringin, but not for me . . . 'I
was standin way back in a corner, alone in a corner of the
whole world, and my heart breakin to see this Willadean
I never knew about.

"After a while I sneaked out and went on home
with the dingdong bells ringin in my head.

"Well, when Willadean got off work and came
home I took her to task for her actions in the C.O.D.

Café and we had a family ruckus good and proper, Willadean shoutin, 'I've got a right to do as I *damned* please. When *you* start tellin *me* what to do, the fat's in the fire. Got me some good men friends here, as good as any you'll find in Houston or anyplace else — *you've* never had any, but *I'm* goin to — and right now my special one is Mr. Steve Cavanaugh, who is an oilman with lots of money and a big Packard . . . .'

"And Mama said, 'Hattie Hattie, Willadean's pretty and popular in the town, not like you was, goin to church and Sundayschool and doin all the chores on the place. Why are you so hateful? Times have changed and ways have changed in Charity, and Willadean has to have her some men friends, she's no little girl anymore . . . .'

"That was all the thanks I got.

"Well, when Willadean got married away to the widower from up at Sanderson I never heard from her much anymore. And there was Gilbert to handle, poor crippled Gilbert up and grown and needin to have braces on his legs so he could walk, since he was paralyzed when jest a little boy by the paralysis plague that hit all the childrun of Charity so hard and killed quite a parcel of em back in the woods. Sent Gilbert to doctors in Houston, paid for his braces, by the month, then sent him to a school up north in Illinois to learn watchmakin.

"But there was nothin I could do with Thrash, just hung around Mama and set on the front porch, never would do a lick a work, like a child, cuddlin close to Mama, warm and close in some dream.

"O Mama and Papa and Willadean and crippled Gilbert and pore old Thrash, ever time I punched the time-clock at the S.P. it 'uz for you.

"What of my time and life I didn't give to all them in Charity, I give to the Church and the Young People in Houston. What times we had! Wienerroasts and bare-footed hikes and hayrides and New Year's Watch Parties. Oh the programs we put on on Sunday nights at Epworth League! The fine speeches made by my boys and girls and the readin out of the Bible verses. The hymns we sang, all of em settin before me, young and bright, Clara Lou Emson, Joe David Barnes, Folner Ganchion, Conchita Bodeen, and all of them, singin loud and joyful 'He Leadeth Me' and 'I Will Be True, for There Are Those Who Trust Me' and our very favrite of all, 'Blest Be The Tie That Binds.' Just for a little while, not long, but just for a wonderful little while, they were all mine, bound to me and bound together, the only thing I ever had, in Fellowship Hall.

"And then they all began to fall away. What ever stays, in this world? One by one, and in such a little while, they drew away and turned from me — to some-thing they had found beyond me and the Epworth League that I could never find — and the Epworth League at the Methodist Church was never the same again.

"It was, I am sure, because all of them went to college and I never had more'n a high school diploma and a bizniss course. This made them take to other interests, the symphony concerts and college clubs, talkin atheism and biology and historical learnin that I never had. I knew they was thinkin, 'Hattie, we've outgrown you,' and on Sunday nights they went to dance at the Rice Hotel instead of comin to League, and on New Year's Eve they was all at the night clubs, and I watched alone. Cept for a few old reliables like Sarah Elizabeth Galt who had a hare-lip, pore thing, and that kind of a sissy Raphael Stevenson, but both good Christians.

"And then a college class was formed at the Methodist Church with Mr. Smart, a college graduate and a prominent lawyer, teachin them. Oh I'm sure he did a good job — but I ask you, is a college graduate a better Christian? Was Jesus a college graduate? These are some things to think about.

"And now there's no one else to help or to call, Hattie Hattie, kin you come home, Hattie Hattie this and Hattie that. Mama and Papa's dead and buried away in Charity and Willadean's raisin her heathen family up in Sanderson and Gilbert's got a good watch-repairin bizniss up north in Deetroit, Michigan. And pore ole Thrash is in the State Home in Orange where he is taken good care of but don't know nothin, nobody. I send things up to him, and onct I went up to see him on the bus, but he never knew who I was, he's gone, in another world. I never go anymore, jes cain't stand it.

"Now all this has passed like a dream and I never go to Charity anymore, cept onct in a while for a funeral of an ole-timer and hear them all say to me, 'I'll swan if tisnt Miss Hattie Clegg — Hattie, remember the old days?' As though I'd jes come *home* to remember them on a weekend . . . That bus I ride home to Charity on, to put flowers on graves at funerals, is a long ride between rememberin and rememberin with nothin but rememberin in between. Here I set in a room I rent from ole Miz Johnson in East End, an old maid left with a twisted face from the Bell's Palsey that struck me like a curse of the Lord six months ago when I was ridin the S.P. on my pass, goin to the Grand Canyon on the first vacation I ever took for myself past Charity Texis as a result of the three weeks they give me at the office for workin twenty-five years with the Southern Pacific. (I get to wear a gold button now, with a 25 on it.) I don't even own my own washrags, everthing round me is rented.

"Why? Why? Benn a Christian all my life. Why, after all this, should I be twisted with a twisted face and no one in the whole wide world to call to me, 'Hattie Hattie . . . ' This is my reward.

"There is a pane of glass between me and the world, seems like, and nothin in the world can ever get to me anymore, only press its nose up against the pane and look through at me. All the world seems flat-nosed against this glass (what breath blows this fog upon my pane?) and I am separated from everthing in the whole world and feel alone and lost and afraid, with no one needin me for anything, useless and twisted and no one dependin on me, callin, 'Hattie Hattie Hattie.' "

O Well! Womb of all my darkness, great dark mouth that swallowed all my agony when you swallowed me. You have held all their faces, mirror of their faces, caught their buckets dropped down like their secret longings deep into themselves, reservoir of all calls and cries of kin: you have lent me to vision, I was borrowed and claimed by some force that wanted to use me in the world for you and never used, wrenched away from you and out of time like an hour out of a clock; I am that bird that walks in the rime of the bog of the icebound bottomlands, chiming his fiery midnight hour, I am Devil, I am Goodness, I am Gall and I am Heartbreak. To be light! light! — to dance like Folner, to hunch in the dark like Swimma, to hear the Ding Dong Bells! O possessions hoarded in a bag with holes, the excrement upon the floor, the clashing of hornéd beaks, the endless sound of hollow shells pouring upon plate, the combinations forming and re-forming, walking up and down under the dripping trees. I am in that staggering timeless moment when vision and life are married in passion and agony in the streets in the rain. A shape, a shape! I see it taking form! That some of us have to find other lives to give our own lives meaning; that we live in others and they live in us; alone on the shingle of the world, washed against this wet rock, O I melt down! Name! Praise! Connect! One molten face forming many faces — I slide down down . . . I start to cry down another name into the well . . . But I hear the shutter's tune in the room where Malley Ganchion sat by the shutter, and I go there. An empty chair sits, as if it were Aunt Malley herself, waiting by the closed shutter. The wind is blowing out a long long tale in the shutter . . . .

IX

HERE YOU SAT, Malley Ganchion, by this old blind window that was like the closed and drooping eye of this decrepit rainwashed house, listening to this sad little tune played by the east wind in the shutter. Pieces of a broken memory drifted by in your head. What was this little lament the wind blew and blows, dipping you (and me) deep down like a bucket into the well of an ancient memoried self? You did everything to stop it, because look what you did to stop it: here in the cracks and louvers are the yellowed stuffed newspapers, the Charity *Clarion*, and the thick cardboard pages with swatches of men's suit material from Sears' catalogue. But nothing stopped that tune in your window when the wind was in the East coming from the Charity River, whirling the cisternwheel and filling the well. You sat and listened and lamented . . . .

"Oh the Charity Riverbottoms where the wind that blows this tune like some mouth on a frenchharp is comin from! There in the spring the dogwood used to blossom and blow, and the rosebud and yella jessmine; and the katdids' ud bleat like the beat of an old rusty heart, and the frogs make such a husky commotion. Oh the sweet breath of the woods—the baby-breath fern and the little woodsviolets and the daylilies; and on Rob's Hill risin up beyond the old river bridge there'd be Fire on the Mountain blazin like the burnin bushes of Moses. There's a new steel bridge now and the old one is broken and swaybacked—the one I'd never ride over, was condemned, and would make them let me get out and walk across when we'd go for our rides out on the Highway. (Remember those summer Sundays we had our picnics there and all'd go wadin in the water, and look for good sweetgum and hickry sticks; and some would be fishin with sugarcane poles and others'd be rustlin through the dry palmettas like fieldmice or stroll-in under the shinin longleaf pines and the blackjack pines—and through it all the sweet little Charity River flowin lazy, and small, and clear as a tear. Instead of all this decoration of the woods, you know what's there now, oilwells there now, thickern flies, all along there; and all the treefrogs and whipperwills are flown away, caint live in an oil derrick, no nature left, no won-der . . .) Nothin is like it used to be except the wind blown from the riverbottoms into my shutter to play a tune about what has gone. (The bottomlands are bald and have sluices and slues full of black, muddy oil scabs, can smell it here when the wind's right. That stink puts all Charity in a spell, they walla in it, it smells money. Never the sweet fresh smell of the old riverbottoms. Is this the vile oil of joy, this green and yellow putrid scum over the ponds?) The world has sold away everything that was beautiful and as the Lord put it here to be, human beins have changed everything into money and show. Why, out by Tomball the lands is littered with oil-well riggins, and day and night the chug-chug-chug and the little flickrin oil flames wavin in the night like the red flags of the Devil staked out to say he owns this infernal land; and nigras and pore people who used to have no more'n one Jersey cow and a few Plymathrock hens got colonial homes and stationwagons. Everything that used to be in East Texis is ruined, there's a terrible change in the world; and I set here left behind in this old house by all my kin and by my dead husband Walter Warren Starnes and my dead daughter Jessy, and my wanderin son Berryben who's gone away through the world and will never come back to me.

"That tune! I try to keep my faith and Job is my example; for I have been smitten with these cataracks on my eyes to test me, it seems, on this dungpile of East Texis. But oh I think the eye of Heaven's got a catarack on it too, gettin blinder and blinder, blinkin and blinkin, closin on the world. Soon it'll be like the dark of the moon, no light, no sight. O Lord wink me over Jordan. O the droopin lid of the sick eye of Heaven, like my own

blighted eyes. Cain't tell who's comin up the road, a
gypsy or a nigra or one of the Cleggs that live over in the
crumblin house. Have to stare and stare at anybody for a
long long look before I can tell who they are, and that
Lulabelle Ramey sayin to me in the Postoffice, 'See anything green, Malley Ganchion?'

"There's a straight pin, I'll pin it in my bosom—see
a pin and pick it up, all the day you'll have good luck; see
a pin and let it lie, all day good luck'll pass you by.

"What is this little tune the wind blows? Listen!
There . . . . It almost played a slow 'Fly in the Buttermilk, Lula, Lula!' but not quite, just enough to torment
me. How we'd dance that tune and clap our hands!
That's a memry! I had a waist neat and limber as a wrist
—and good teeth. I've got pictures that show it, to prove
it to myself; didn't always have this bag hangin down
from my left side, this tumor big as Granny Ganchion's
goiter, this windgall, this big Devil's snuff-box.

"Sometimes when I was young, in the mornins, I
would come to this very shuttered window and think
that if I flung it open wide and quick I might.see before
me a magic world I had never known before, somewhere
out beyond the Katy rayroad tracks and far across
Bailey's Pasture where now there are only cows eatin the
bitterweeds. Then when I'd make a wish and open the
winda wide—there was only the wood-roofed little
shanties of Charity across the pasture and a string of
sickgreen smoke windin out of the sawmill smokestack.

And at night in the summertimes the half-shutter of a small moon in the roof of the Charity sky seemed like if it twas opened, something magic and bright might fly down out of Heaven through it and rescue us all. From what? Poverty and grievin? Oh I don't know, now . . . Sometimes when Walter Warren and I would be sleepin here I would suddenly be wakened by a flood of light swimmin and tremblin upon my face and it would be the bright little moon passin over this house and over us in bed in it and over Bailey's Pasture which it turned silver and white (I see the moon and the moon sees me, God bless the moon and God bless me). And I would lie next to Walter Warren feelin haunted and full of some nightmare, fearin for all of us—Lauralee and her family, Granny Ganchion and all hers, all of us in this old house.

"But Walter Warren would never save me from anything of fear or any nightmare. The world he gave me was cold; and so I waited for you, Berryben, to grow up and make the world warm and save something for me.

"Walter Warren would never let me swank. When I had my hair bobbed (was one of the first of Charity to do it, sittin on a crate on the back screenporch), Esther Crow came over to do it and I was so excited, trembled and giggled and I screamed so and we all got so tickled (something terrible happened) and me screamin so, 'Oh! oh! oh!', that it scaired little Berryben half to death and he cried, 'Mama! Mama!' and thought they were hurtin me and ran and hit Esther Crow and tried to pull her away from me to protect me and Walter Warren was mad and trembled too and went away to set on the front porch sayin 'I'll be damned, Malley'; and little Berryben ran cryin out to the chickenyard.

"Then Walter Warren would grumble about my long gloves I'd wear at nights over my coldcreamed hands and arms to keep them white—for him, but he never cared. But he cared enough to make me have Jessy, me in my condition that never should have had another child and she was born so hard and mangled and nearly killed me; that's why she died so young, because she never should have been born.

" 'That's right,' I would say to Walter Warren, lyin with his back to me in the night, 'wait til Ben grows up, we'll never have to depend on you for anything.'

"And I'd lie there and hear the tune in the shutter and feel cold and alone and want to die except for Berryben, my salvation, in the next room, sleepin with his little sickly sister Jessy.

"It was waitin and waitin, through these cold years. And then, when it was time, Berryben just turned and went away and I cain't ever call him back. It was Walter Warren drove him away, that meanness in him; called him a scoundrel once, always criticized him and fought with him at the supper table, made him vomit up all his supper, is why he was always so thin.

"Here at this very winda little Berryben stood with

me once and watched the tents and folks of a circus that
had crept in one night to the pasture while we all slept—
it was like some fairytale thing; and I wanted to go but
Walter Warren wouldn't, so Berryben and I and Folner
went and we bought a red and yellow paper bird that
whistled when the wind turned him on a stick. And
again one morning when I opened this very winda I
discovered the big flappin tent of those Holy Rollers that
had just cropped up like a toadstool in the night and
stayed and stayed until the fool preacher was bit and
killed by the sting of a diamond rattler whose poison he
swore to all Charity the Lord would antidote through
prayer. Then the tent was moved away. I'd lie and hear
their shoutin songs and sit and watch the cripples come
on their crutches and in wheelchairs to be healed—and
some of them were, too; threw away their crutches and
walked away. That young Jempson boy did.

"Walter Warren and I strolled and courted in that
very pasture and walked the rayroad ties under the
moon.

"Now there are only cows in the bitterweeds.

"The whole time of my life has been in this house in
this town. Seems I have seen my whole world through
this stereoscope of a winda. Often I sat sewin and darnin
here in the summers, the summer sun slantin in and lyin
on my hands and gleamin the needle (and a little golden
stair of golden dust archin up and out through the winda
that might be a golden ladder up to somethin) and

watched through this very winda the children playin out
in the pasture across the Katy tracks, chasin and cryin in
their games. Berryben flew a kite there in the March
winds and the sight of that little thing holdin on hard to
a flyin kite with all his might is a memry of him. Or
watched the children walkin the rayroad ties or swinging in and out on the iron gate; and singin in the yard, 'I
measure my love to show you.' And another time a wild
black bull upon a cow in the pasture and the children
screamin, in November. Once Berryben brought me in a
rain-soaked and smeared doll's head from the pasture
that he had lost and searched for there, and I made a little
rag and sawdust body for it, and there it sets on that sofa
to this very day, next to the pilla from Hawaya that
cousin Sewall who joined the Navy sent.

"But when all my sorrow came I closed this shutter
and've never opened it again. Why should I? I'd only see
the Katy tracks and the haunted pasture beyond — and I
feel like I don't want to ever lay eyes on it again through
this winda. Sometimes the eastern sun tries to worm
through the blinds and I almost want to open them; but
then I don't and never will again. When Berryben went
out that front gate I said, 'It's only for a little while and
he'll be back, don't grieve so, Malley Ganchion.'

"I watched him walk straight across the pasture on
the path to town and played like he was only goin to the
store for meat and chicken feed. So straight and quick,
walkin across Bailey's Pasture, he went, with his

suitcase, goin to take a temporary job in Nackadoches, he said. Little Jessy waved at the fence and I waved from this winda. Walter Warren stayed out in the patch and would not look or say good-bye. He and I was all alone together with just little sickly Jessy. Lauralee and Jimbob had gone to live with Maidie in Dallas while Lauralee had her teeth pulled (but then she died suddenly there before they could ever come back) and Swimma had gone to Dallas, too, and started her shameful life.

"Then every day I'd set and set by this winda watching for Berryben. It was fall and the leaves and the leaves were fallin and I thought the leaves must leave their tree when it is time, how sad to see them leave the mother tree. But they will come back, too, in their right time, I said.

"All the winter I waited and watched; and the spring come quick, the way it does here, and the dogwood trail was all white again and redbud abloom by the riverbottoms and the leaves came sure enough back but not Berryben. Of course I know that that Evella Sykes had gone to him but I didn't allow what I thought to anyone, even to Walter Warren, I kept what I thought to myself. She was older than him and had had one husband who had died in Charity, and she was a kind of mother to him, I know, loved him and wanted to help him all she could. He never mentioned her to me in his letters.

"Then years passed, and in one of these that passed

Jessy fell so quickly sick and passed on so quickly with that one year . . . . Berryben wrote me a letter sayin he couldn't come, on account of his bein so far away and had obligations there.

"And then word come to me that Evella Sykes had gone away from Ben and that that was all over.

"So quick Walter Warren passed on, going as silent to his grave as he had always been here on the place, keeping some secret to himself that he would never tell. I never knew how sick he'd been until they said he died of a cancer.

"Then Maidie wanted me to come on to Dallas and live with them; but they had trouble enough and I didn't want to live in a city and I wanted to stay in this old house. And here I've stayed. Some of the Cleggs come over once in a while to see if I am all right. That good Hattie's been gone for years, works in Houston but comes home once in a while; and the young ones have scattered into trouble and scandal, and only the old Cleggs live there in that house that I declare to the Lord will fall right in on them one day.

"Hope the wind don't get in the flue, cain't stand *that* sound . . . . There is twilight in this house. Oughtn't to be so alone, goin to get me some boarders.

"That tune! Now it sounds like pore Jessy's voice singin like she used to — 'Rescue the Perishing' (Rescue the perishing, care for the dying, Jesus is merciful, Jesus will save . . .) at our Mason piano in the living room that was ruined by the leak in the roof over it and the rain gave it such a clinkety tune (Berryben wanted to play that old piano so, but Walter Warren would fuss and fume and rant so when he caught him at it that finally the little thing made a keyboard out of a cardboard and hid out in the woodshed playin cardboard music that nobody could hear). Pitiful little runted Jessy, stunted by what curse of the Lord? Just too frail to live through a life, just at nineteen death took her away (to a better land I know); but oh how she lay so coppercolored in that bed for days and days, moanin and moanin, somethin like this sound in the shutter now — and the day she died I heard the rumblin of a wagon on the road and the mournful terrible call of old Mr. Hare through his nose: 'paa-ahs! paa-ahs!'; and while his call was still in my head Jessy breathed so hard and died away from all of us. It was her liver. (The children would always run and hide when old Mr. Hare would pass callin. 'Old Mr. Hare will get you,' I would say when they were ugly and mean.)

"Jessy, Jessy, I put out all your pictures sometimes, get a mania for em. Take spells when I jest need to see you so. Sometimes it's a baby picture of you 'th not a hair on your little head and a little golden locket hangin round your frail little neck. Sometimes it's that one of you and Berryben standin together by the speckled yellow canna; then the one of you in your pale girlhood jest at sixteen in your sateen blouze that I worked orange

curlimakews in for you. You looked like a little elf, never
was of this world, taken from the beginnin. Then I put
em all away again, back in my goods box, back with all
your little clothes and Sunday-school things, after I get
my fill of em. Those little biddy softsoled shoes! The
print of your little feet was no bigger than a mock-
ingbird's. Many times I think you was the only good
thing sent among us, so good and frail and gentle, never
hurt a fly.

    "Seems like I've so little now, seems like I'm nothin
at all, useless and idle and old and blind, that I have to
get out signs and tokens of all I've been and done in my
life to prove that once I'uz somethin more. Then I go to
the watery mirror in the hall by the hat-tree and look at
myself and see my droopin cataracted eyes and it appears my face is all meltin down, cryin down in tears and
meltin away like Epaminondas' butter. Oh my! How we
can come to so little from so much in this life, wouldn't
believe it if you didn't have pictures to prove it. Oh the
memry of the catbrush of you and Berryben against my
legs as I stood at the kitchen woodstove that I will never
feel again . . . All of it seems like a dream, like a trance,
a woman old and blind as me shouldn't be alone so long.
Sometimes I get in a spell, there's such a long chain of
days, one like the other goin on and on and on, till it
seems I don't know any time or place or anything and
even the clocks go all wrong and seem to tell no time and
I feel like a cork that bobbles and drifts in a pond. And I

go through room and room and say to myself *'what muss I do? but what muss I do?'* and pass like a graveyard of memry all the signs of everbody gone and all the relics of you all, and I stand by the well and look down to see my face and want to cry into the well, 'Who are you, can you be Malley Ganchion, *who are you?'* and pass the watery mirror that quivers my dissolving face like a face seen in the well, shimmerin and runnin together to form Berryben's, then Jessy's, then Lauralee's, then even Granny's and Folner's faces; and even look out the kitchen winda for somebody to pass on the road and see only one lone black buzzard sailing high and slow and quiet over sawmill town. (See one buzzard, don't see two, you'll see someone you're not expectin' to.) and then 'paa-ahs! paa-ahs!', comes the ancient wail of old hare-lipped Mr. Hare selling pears from his wagon. And finally I end up at this winda and set and remember all over again and get everthing straight and get hold of my-self again.

"Now the wind is Jessy's voice just as plain. Listen."

"Hello, Mama, I've got a little talking to do, too.

"I always knew I wouldn't last. Know how I knew I was sick? Had that pain always down in my side but never told about it. And lots of times, at night, I'd lie in my bed and see a sight; and when they were burning brush over by the river it was a signal of some kind to

me; and most of all when I sang my hymns at the piano I
knew I wouldn't last, that I was called. ('Hear the soft
whisper wherever you are. From this sad world He
would take you apart; Tenderly calling: Give me thy
heart!') I was always hearing the soft whisper. When I
would be hiding behind the pyrocanthus bush in a
game some little ticking bug would be ticking in the
bush and seemed to be telling a secret time for me. Or
when I would be doing homework by the woodstove in
the kitchen I would hear the little bugle blowing in the
woodstove, it was a call of a faroff land, calling me ('Softly and tenderly Jesus is calling, Calling to you and to me,
Calling Oh sinner come home. Come home, come ho-o-
ome; Ye that are weary come ho-o-ome . . . ')

"There were so many signs. At night the sight of
the three black hens sitting in the beantree when I would
go out to the privy with a lantern was like three black angels waiting for me. And the knocking of the fiery-eyed
moths at the window, staring at me by the lamplight
they craved and fluttering against the pane, their
terrible burning faces — it seemed they wanted me and
not the light.

"In church the women singing in the pews, the sad
strained voices and the wailing screaming voices
calling, 'Rescue the Perishing.'

"In church the long yellow face of Brother Ramsey
crooked over the pulpit and hovering over us in the
congregation like a scarey falseface on a stick, clacking

his gray teeth over us like the rattle of bones, saying, 'And the Lord will open the Book on Judgment Day and the Lord will read out the names written there. Chuck Adams, will *your* name be written there in the Book?'

"And the congregation trembled and somebody shouted in the silence 'Hep him, Lord!'

"We all wanted our names in the Book, prayed and worshiped and tithed and took communion to get our names written there.

"My special flower was the little go-to-sleep flower and I loved it most of all. I knew where a bunch of them lived in our pasture and would often go there and lay my finger on their leaves and put them asleep. (And at the Chatauqua I wore my red crepepaper dress that you made for me, Mama; and Berryben, who was some kind of clown with a pointed cap, spurted water from a fountain on me and my dress melted down. But he didn't mean to. And at the May Fete I was a flower and Berryben a King with a silver crown and a wand and silver stars on it made out of Dennison paper. When Berryben the King wove in and out all us flowers squatting low with heads bent over, he quietly touched all the flowers with his silver wand and all the flowers lifted up and bloomed. But when he touched me I was so excited and wanted to be so ready to bloom up — and his touch was like an angel touching me, so gentle — that I felt paralyzed for a minute and couldn't bloom, and then fell to the ground; and all the people laughed.)

"I loved all the yellow roses by the woodshed, how in the springtime the very air round the woodshed was stained and flushed golden by all the yellow roses. (But I never put one in my hair, I cross my heart I never; I never prissed, I never sinned that way; I never had vanity, vanity or wanted any lipstick. If I'd have lived, I'd a had a wart on my nose, anyway, and it would a sprouted a bristle like all the Ganchion women have.) I wanted to go to Heaven, to the city Foursquare and paved with gold that we sang about in church and that Brother Ramsey told us over and over again about; to have my name in the Book, Mama.

> " 'Wire, briar, limberlock
> Three geese in a flock;
> One flew east
> And one flew west
> And one flew over the cuckoo's nest.'

"You see how much I knew, Mama, that you never knew? I was just everywhere and all the time called and I was not afraid but really glad, for the Methodist Church had prepared me and I had always prayed long and hard at night or any time when I needed the help and strength of prayer; and I knew my Redeemer would take me to him when he needed me. So I was not scared. You know yourself, Mama, that I was born with a veil over my face, that I was stunted and stunned at birth and Miz Van and

Pollyella Van had to hold me first in a tub of hot water and then a tub of cold to get my circulation running. You know that I was purple for three days and nights, that nobody ever thought I'd live.

"I played with the littler children out in the yard, hopscotch and Teacher on the front steps and Crack the Whip and Drop the Handkerchief (and when I ran too hard I would wipe away some blood from my nose and I would go away to hold my blood in my hand and look at it and wonder what it meant; but I never told); and Jacks in the hall when it rained. We called to Doodle-bugs, using the straw of a broom.

" *'How many hearses shall I have? One two three four five six . . .*

"About Berryben, Mama. He always stood up for me and now I want to stand up for him. Let him go around or if he's hiding, let him hide. He's trying to dive down for something to bring up for us all to see and to save us by. I hope we can all bear to face it when he brings it up. He wants to touch us all for all our sakes, Mama, for all our sakes, where we can bloom, and burst us up open into light. Everything else wants to touch us and close us up and put us to sleep.

"He was always so gentle, never hurt me once in our games, always gave up to me. If we both had a syrup biscuit I would eat mine quick and then say 'havers' and get half of his. He would never fuss for this. He always saved his good things back — to give away when and if they were asked for. That, I believe, is what he's doing now; finding some real good thing to give away one day when it is asked for or needed.

"Once he built a little house out of croakersacks for me and my dolls and when me and my dolls were cozy inside our good house, Berryben set it on fire and I burned off some of my hair, but I didn't get mad, that was all right, it was because Berryben's wagon was supposed to be a fire wagon and needed a fire to put out and I understood.

"And then we kept secrets; and buried pretty little pieces of broken glass for treasure and never told anyone where they were hid.

"We all wanted to bury him and save him back like a little buried treasure for ourselves always. But so many things came early to claim him away from us, for themselves. He had a special place to go, just as I had. But always, when good and special things want you, just as many bad and ugly things crave you too; and there is a battle on. Berryben is in some battle.

"Oh I don't mean to sound so smart, but you must understand that I have got some wisdom from this death. We were just lost here, Mama, where you sit by your closed window. We didn't know where to go, but we wanted to go away from Charity and the sawmill. The Church told me where to go and got me ready — for I was marked for death when I was born. Berryben chose some other place that we can't understand yet but will.

"And I got this death, Papa's got his, you got these cataracks and this lonesome grieving life, and Berryben has his hiding away and searching. But he'll redeem us all, in the end. I know he will. He only wants us all to wait and we will finally understand. He's good, Mama. He's a good thing live in this world, that's gone but coming back twofold.

"But we never had any life together, all of us, you and me and Berryben and daddy. Daddy was so alone, all to himself, and you would stand away from us at the window, looking away from us, grieving always for something out beyond the window and beyond us. And Berryben had his own world, we could never touch him or gather him to us. And I had my secret signs. We were all looking for something and I wonder what?

"Not long ago I dreamt I was home again in Charity with you all and that I went out by the cisternwheel and found no water there because the cisternwheel had fallen to the ground and the well had dried, and that it was the end of all our time and sorrow and sinning because the oilwells and evil had come to Charity in a time of great drought, drying up the river, and there were no more birds, only a great pest of grasshoppers that had flown into all the gardens and eaten up the crops, and Charity was filled with freaks and tarred running Negroes, and Charity hated Jews and Charity hated Yankees and Charity even hated Charity, and everybody good was gone. And that the sawmill had

grown so big and so close to our house that all day the
sawdust sifted down on our yard, in our house, choking
us, like white Fuller's Earth at Riverside. And that the oil
money had bred swank and greed and false-facedness
and we were all playing a game and deceiving ourselves
and deceiving and cheating others and would not look at
our true selves because we did not have the courage to
endure what we would find; and that all things fell to
pieces like the broken wheel. And that when I looked
down by the broken wheel I saw the little leaves of my
go-to-sleep flower and said softly 'Go to sleep.' And the
little leaf folded together.

"But don't grieve, poor blind and lonesome Mama.
We have our Redeemer."

"Jessy, Jessy, you speak only a memry in my shutter and I can hear it just as plain. But I can't think
straight, too old and blind and mixed up. I can only hear
your voice like a wind in my shutter. But now — hear it?
The wind is singing in the shutter about Berryben, pore
lost and sufferin Berryben. Oh Berryben Berryben I
lighted the way leadin home a hundred times that winter you was over in Sour Lake, burnt the coaloil lamps
late; but you would never see any road that led back to
Charity and this house.

" 'But I can't come back to Charity, Mama,' you
wrote from Sour Lake. 'What is there in Charity for me?
Can't anybody do *anything*, go *any*wheres? I got to keep

moving, can't stop, can't settle, like a bee in a flower bed.'

"And then I had a letter from Saren saying you had moved on there.

" 'But Charity's as good a place as any on this earth,' I said. 'Got the foundry, got a new plant of some kind out by White Rock and also goin to get a paper mill factory; lots of nice young people, all askin about you, ought to see what a time they have. Come on home to Charity where your own blood is and settle down and make your way.'

"But you would never come, I could have preached to you till the world looked level but you would never never come; kept movin and movin over Texis, blown like a tumbleweed — by what wind, what wind, Berryben? And now, hearin this tune blown by the wind in the winda, I think of you next, my pore lost and sufferin little Berryben. What was there that made you different from us all? A mother's got the right to understand her own son even though the whole rest of the world don't and cain't. But you would never come close where I could really set down and ask you face to face what was it? What was it made you different? Was it your father that wouldn't let you play the piano or be anything that hounded and scaired you? Was it your Granny Ganchion that put some Ganchion curse in your blood and set such an example for you? If I could have just seen you, I could have read it in your face, whether you and

Evella Sykes were in love and why she followed you round. But I swore I would never mention her name again to you or even say her name again to myself.

"We could never hold you, none of us. You seemed like a little scaired animal of some kind. Somethin somewhere had shaken you up, scaired you so that nobody could ever hold you still. You trembled. Was it Evella Sykes, or was it Charity or was it all of us you got ashamed of and ran away from — your own blood an bones?

"Come on home, it's not too late, even after all these years. The light's on. Haven't been home in Charity for years and years, not even to lay a wreath on your dead sister Jessy's grave nor set a pot of geraniums on your daddy's. I remember everthing you ever said to me, that the world is big and Charity so small and this house old and sleepy. I've kept em all in my heart and pondered them, all the words you said. How it nearly killed me at first, really it did, I vow to you Berryben it nearly killed me, couldn't even swallow water. Had to keep busy mornin to night workin and doin; if ever I'd a set down I'd a burst out cryin. When there was no chores to be done, before I had my cataracks, I'd embroidry. Embroidried twelve cup towels that winter you left, one right after another.

"I knew you wanted somethin that we all didn't know about; and you kept it secret from me and would never let me know. That you wanted to go out after somethin in the world — somethin that your father never found but maybe grieved for. And I didn't know how to tell you how to do it, Berryben; I would have helped you if I could've, Lord knows I would've, would've done anything. You were my hope, boy Ben, when you went away all my hope went with you. You were my only chanct. *You* closed this winda on my world, and when the wind comes from the riverbottoms there's the song of all this sorrow between you and me in the shutter; the song of sorrow in the shutter's the same as in my mind. You were my only chanct. For what? I'm not sure, I cain't say anymore, I'm all confused and riled up inside, cain't say; but in you there seemed to be all my chance for everything. But I couldn't keep you; anyway I tried, I couldn't keep you. When you went away I said I know it's right that you go, wouldn't have you stay at all if you don't want to stay, want you to do what you have to do, what will make you happy Ben, I won't keep you. But what I felt when I found out you were *never* comin back I can never tell you, just the whole insides of me gone and fallen to pieces.

"Our life was so hard and so little, I knew you would make it big for us — sneaked money to you for your expression lessons with that teacher that came in onct a week from Huntsville — all this behind your daddy's back to get you out of the sawdust, Berryben, to deliver you from the sawmill, to put you in a better world and away from the trash standin round in striped

shirts and bigbilled caps on Saturday nights in front of
Duke's Drug Store with cigarettes hangin out of their
mouths.

"You were such a promise in the church. I thought
you would give your life to the church and for the good
of mankind. I still believe you uz called to be a preacher
and Hattie Clegg does too. How you can do this to us all I
don't understand.

"But what do I have? Only the twilight of this old
memry-house, and a chickensnake's somewhere in the
castorbeans stealin my few eggs, and settin by this shuttered winda listenin to this tune playin out my memry
by a wind from the ruined Charity Riverbottoms.

"Berryben and Jessy, my two pore lost children, listen, listen to the wind's tune. Your pore old daddy,
Walter Warren Starnes, for a long time after both you left
us he never slept well, slept hardly at all, set up quick in
his bed at nights and couldn't get his breath. Said he was
chokin, said it was his heart; but I know it was memry
and worry over you had their hands at his throat and his
heart. Parents oughtn't to do that, I know, but how else
can you do? Then he'd hear a noise in your rooms and
say, 'Malley, there's a sound a footsteps comin from
Berryben's room, *he's come home*'; or, 'Malley, there's
some commotion in Jessy's room'; and he'd take the
shotgun and go creepin and a pointin it through every
room, all through your room, Ben, and all through your
room, Jessy; and I would lie there, frozen, thinkin, what

find, an excaped convick from the Pen at Huntsville or a
rat or just the creakin floor, but never Ben or Jessy. And
there was never nothin in your rooms, never nothin at
all but everthing standing left the way you left them,
quiet and like you left them. I'd lie there in my bed and
want to die, and think — is this what parents have to
come to, a creepin at night through room and room with
a shotgun after the ghosts of their children who've gone
away and left them lonely and sleepless and chokin in
the night? O the memry of your daddy in his nightshirt
creepin through your deserted rooms with a shotgun in
his hands!

"This house is like an old burnt-out hollow of a
tree. Why should a mother have to set midst all the
heartbreakin leftovers of the past? Goin to rent out these
rooms, goin to move to the City Hotel, or write to Cousin
Lottie in Lovelady to come and stay with me.

"The Lord hep us and bind us.

"You used to write me not to think so much,
Berryben; but I must look back, pillar of salt or no. And
that wind turns a slow and steady wheel through the waters of my memry as it blows this tune of sorrow in my
shutter. O what's the meanin of it all? There *must* be *some*
meanin somewhere — it cain't all be just this
rabblement and helter-skelter. *Somethin* has to replace
what's lost in us, what's grown and been harvested or
withered, like crops — but what? We are taken and held
and shaken by so many things in life; but in the end it is

Memry that gets us — we are finally delivered into the
bitter, clawin hands of Memry after life is through
handlin us and is done with us. We ought to see to it that
we make good memry for ourselves, like a slow and
perfect stitchin, as we go along, and embroidry a good
and lovely memry out of all the thread we one day have
to set, alone, and unravel, stitch by stitch. Now I see that
every day I uz makin a memry and didn't know it. Oh
wish I uz like old Aunt Mat Bell — she cain't remember a
thing, cain't even remember her name — everthing that
ever was, for her, is gone, wiped clean out of her head.
'Molly Jim,' she'll say to her daughter, 'what's my name,
Molly Jim?' Seems like a blessed state.

   "But listen! Listen — wind sounds just like
Berryben talkin . . . "

   "Listen again, Mama, and I'll try to tell you for the
hundredth time what it was that made me go away."
   "I'm listenin, Ben, but let me see your face. I cain't
see your face, Berryben."
   "It's because you don't open the shutter, Mama,
because you'll never open the shutter. But let me tell you
if I can. *I really left so I could come back again.*"
   "But it'll be too late, then. Either I'll be too blind to
see your face or I'll be dead and gone."
   "It's never too late to come back again, Mama.
There was just something that called me away from the
Sundays on the porch and the children in the yard, from

the grieving and misery and bitterness of Aunty and Granny Ganchion, from the scrape and rusty screech of the cisternwheel. It called me when I sat in the black hen's tree, when I stood in the fields, when I thumped on my cardboard piano in the woodshed. There seemed something more magnificent than the Charity loneliness. Somewhere there would be somebody to understand me — I could prove my blood — feel and find out the keys of a piano that *played*, not just a dumb-show. But more: an unnameable call away from all the withered quiet and dying old life and ways of this little world of Charity, hemmed in by a railroad track and a sawmill and a deserted meadow.

"All I know is that there was a change in me and, discovering that change in me, I would do anything to keep it unchanged, I would not let it die in me. I had to keep listening, listening, listening to it, just as you listen to another thing in this shutter. The sawmill tried to drown it out, the cisternwheel tried to drown it out; I had to save it, hear it; so I went away. I don't want to live if I can't hear that voice. When I was home you followed me round through the rooms saying, 'If you'll just tell me what is wrong with you! What is changing you, if you'll just put me straight on it all, Ben?'

"And when I would wipe you away then it would break my heart and break your heart and you would catch my face in your hands as if you could hold me there forever, caught in your poor old hands, and weep and say, 'Ben Ben Berryben'; and then I knew that I could never tell you what it was, only break your heart again and again.

"I tricked you all to get away, but I couldn't tell the truth about the things that claimed me. Because you always said these things were sins. I always had that terrible guilt before you, had to tell lies and lies — *you really made me evil*, you made me be just what you were afraid I'd be. I served you all and let you all use me any way you wanted; anything you wanted me to be I was. Took care of little Jessy day in and day out. I never had any romance except because of what Folner and Christy and Swimma told me like a secret. (Once when we sat on the fence rail in the late afternoon, Swimma said, 'Look!' and it was the bull upon Roma the cow in some savage battle and when I said, 'The bull will kill Roma the cow!' Swimma laughed on the fence and leaned over and told me. Later she wrote a word on the chimney brick and couldn't erase it, and I would see those letters written on the walls of the bedroom and on the ceiling, everywhere, smudged the way Swimma's hand had smudged them. I never fully understood until we pumped in the swing, first me then Swimma, and then I suddenly knew the whole terrible secret. After that when Swimma would cry, 'Pump me! Pump me!' I would tremble.)

"Sometimes, because I am a failure in the world, I blame my failure on you all; say that you got me so mixed up when I was young that I can never clear myself up again inside; or that you made me so false to myself that I am unreal and never can be real. But I must see that the reason I am a failure is that I gave myself away to everybody and so had none of myself left for myself — I mean the part of oneself that is the part he works with, held by himself to work with.

"And yet I collaborated with you in making myself false — for I was so afraid of myself and what it wanted to do, and so ashamed of it. So you and I together stomped the life out of it, every day, mangling it like a beetle.

"But suddenly something beyond all of us, greater than all of us, freed us from each other. We tore at our hearts because we were powerless against this thing that came in between us and wrenched us apart. This was loving somebody.

"She came, gentle and sweet, bringing peace, at a time when I was the loneliest and most miserable boy in the world. She made all my secrets vanish into her. For she made me feel that everything I had kept secret was kept back just to tell her — we were joined within a secret that was divulged to us by touching where we had never touched before, and by the honesty of passion where we had been dishonest before. After our honesty with each other, what more was there to hide? We had told. Passionate love is a conspiracy to tell each other's truth to each other — that I am like this and you are like

that, and together, in a joining, we make a moment's
truth of what each is. Beyond the moment's truth,
though, lies the hour's untruth, which keeps yearning to
be bared into truth again. She broke my unreality
against her reality like a pot dashed against a stone, and
mended me with all the care in the world, it seemed. For
her I betrayed you and for myself I betrayed her; we
melted into each other. I tricked you and left you: and after I had left you, all your kin and all your world died
away from you and fell away, leaving you broken off and
isolate. All of us were shattered from our whole, I roam-
ing through the world with Evella, you sitting by the
window trying to piece everything together again in a
falling house.

"That very meadow upon which you close your
shutter was a pasture of revelation, of trembling news
for me. For it was enchanted, some grass of magic grew
there, could it have been the bitterweed? When the circus came, Folner and you and I went — just across the
tracks, there it was: the lovely sparkling girls whirling in
the air like stars. And the times I played there — all the
things I found when I played there brought me secret
news: once a curled transparent skin; the evening prim-
roses, hairy and firm, opening and closing at the touch
of light or darkness; the doll was lost there and later
found, but found too late, trodden and mangled and
broken by Roma the cow. After the circus left to go
across the river and into the world, stealing Folner with

it like a gypsy steals a painted bead, I went there and found sawdust all over the meadow (and got sawdust in my shoes) and all the secret signs left by the magic circus; but the bitterweeds grew up *through* the sawdust, Mama. And Evella and I walked through the bitterweeds on summer nights (scattering the pollen and gathering it on our legs), I telling her about my hopes and she saying, 'I will follow you across the river and past Riverside.'

"What did we go after? I can't tell you. What do you yearn after, here at the window? *Something marvelous, something magic, that makes all secrets vanish.*

(When the forlorn beast, the spotted heifer Roma, bellowed at dusk in the wet meadow, it was a mystic desire, a voluptuous fear, a call way into the future, beyond the meadow, beyond Charity, over the River and far beyond — the voice of Bailey's Pasture. That wintertime, standing by the window, I worried about the poor cow caught in the ditch. The gray, dull winter was everywhere, in the eaves where icicles hung like daggers, in the naked trees and across the bare dead earth where life lay frozen and paralyzed. That wintertime, standing by the window and looking out upon the winter and behind me you, Mama, singing softly 'Pass me not, O gentle Savior, Hear my humble cry'; as you sewed something, rocking in a chair. The loneliness of standing looking out a window at winter upon a town, feeling afraid, like crying, while you Mama, sat in this room sewing and singing.

> 'While on others Thou art calling,
> Do not pass me by . . . '

And the poor spotted cow out there, frozen in the ditch, the way she bellowed and called out for them to help her, to break her out of the ice ('Mama,' I said, 'they are coming with axes. Mama,' I said, 'they will kill her, Roma the cow; Mama,' I said, 'they cannot get her out of the frozen ditch and oh she cries, she cries so sadly').

"The low pleading bellows of Roma came through the window on the winter wind and I felt sick with it all, the room, you, Mama, singing and sewing in that chair as if nothing were happening, the winter spread over everything outside, killing everything, the men (Christy was the leader) with the axe over the poor ugly cow Roma caught in the ice. ('Mama,' I said, 'she is crying so loud, now, like the dog the time he was sick under the house. Mama!' I cried, 'they have hit her hard on the head with the axe, hard! hard! hard! Mama — she is quiet, now; Mama — she is not crying anymore. Mama . . . Roma the cow is dead.'

"But you kept on singing softly softly

> 'Savior, Savior, Hear my humble cry;
> While on others Thou art calling,
> Do not pass me by.')

"Evella and I wandered and wrote you occasionally. I was in a beautiful spell. It was in an autumn and it was a turning round, through light and darkness, under suns and stars, in a fantasy land. The faces of days were disaster and passion. The luminous wind was binding the autumn to the glistening world, blowing it round through trees with a sound of the breaking sea, and the sun was driving summer away, weaving autumn into the world and turning a wheel in Evella and me, turning us towards and turning us away — all love is a turning on a spit, towards, through, and away from flame — and we were like sleepwalkers and Evella would turn to me and say, 'Who are you?' And I would murmur, 'I am you and you are me and we are some rabblement of soul . . .

"With Evella I could never see myself, only hold up a mirror for Evella to see herself; thus I became unreal. Who has the courage to destroy the one who makes him unreal? We parted; and she rolled away like a stone into an abyss. Now I had only myself to remake. I was alone and floating in the world; and I was alien to Charity and felt I never could return to all those secrets — the passion of the Bull, Swimma's news of trembling, Christy's songs and stories and his scar, the blood of his killed creatures . . .

"The world is a window fogged by my own breath through which I cannot see the world because of my own

breath upon the pane; and until I wipe it away with this
ragged sleeve, I shall not see what lies beyond the window; nor you, Mama. We spend our youth breaking the
enchantments of childhood; it is the bitterest time of all.
Youth is the naked, disenchanted child, shivering without garment; for the garments of childhood fall into
ashes.

"Of all the evils you taught and tried to teach me,
the *only* evil is that we cut ourselves off from any force
that wants to flow into us and use us like a turbine; or
that when that force finds us we hold ourselves still,
blind and deafen ourselves to it. The finding of that
force, the awareness of it, quivering in us, trying to turn
us so that we may generate, and the attempt to use it is to
make oneself real. The substitution of any other force is a
mechanical turning and is false; is evil.

"To belong to this force does not make me evil or a
failure at all, it only gives me back to you, to all of you,
Evella and all of you whom I have ever loved or who have
ever loved me; only restores me to you.

"Oh it is a crooked path I follow, Mama, but a
straight wisdom comes from it once in a while; and once
in a while a sure and beautiful joy comes from it and I
will build my life on that wisdom and on that joy that
comes once in a while. And give it all back to you and
those who follow you, to mend all that is ruined and
broken.

"O the drone of the flies and the bees droning in the

zinnias like a sound blown by a child on a comb and a piece of tissue-paper; and the melancholy working of the wind in the trees and a whole dead town gleaming out before us in a false serenity under the burning sun of a fleecy summer Sunday sky with a piece of a moon in it, and nothing happening.

"Mama open your eyes; open the shutter, Mama. For surely one day I'll come back to this house. And what will that terrible, terrible moment be like when the shutter will open slowly like the unfolding of a waking go-to-sleep flower and there is beheld before you the wide shining meadow of Bailey's Pasture, yellow with blooming sweetclover and spotted with a thousand trembling bees — and through it on the old path will be coming me, wading as if I were wading in to a shore through shallows of the sea, home; and with gifts in my hands.

"What will that terrible moment be like when you, blind from cataracts, will sit on there, never knowing that the shutter is open, with the tune playing on in your head; blind for so long that suddenly when vision comes restored you go on blind and yearning and wailing for the vision?

"Hear me, Mama? Hear me in the shutter?"

But Malley Ganchion you went on sitting there with the wind's tune in your head and said, "Let me see your face, Ben; I want to see your face; I want to catch and hold it in my hands."

But no answer came.

And when no answer came, you sat and said, "Oh I wait for somethin to come to me, just as I expected it when long ago I flung open this winda in the mornin upon Bailey's Pasture; and I guess it must be the peace of Death I am waitin for and was always waitin for, to come callin like old hare-lipped Mr. Hare from his rumblin wagon, 'Paa-ahs! paa-ahs!' And oh I am old and tired and left behind by all I gave everthing I ever had to, and I want to die and pass away from all this eternal task of memry and heartbreak and never remember, never remember again.

"And now listen — the voices have gone, and only the little tune remains, playin that beautiful and peaceful hymn of the Methodist Church, 'Oh Let Us Pass over the River and Rest Under the Shade of the Trees.' "

X

FOLNER was sad and cheap and wasted, a doll left in the rain, a face smeared and melted a little, soft and wasted and ruined. Where did he go when he crept away in the nighttime, staying sometimes for two or three days, then returning spent and wasted and ruined a little in his face?

Now ruin returning to ruin come, purged of that spleen and blood of passion (into the empty purity of peace), come through Bailey's Pasture (Beauty's changed Beast) over the railroad track and home — who had lapped with bestial tongue the riverwater at the river, the blood of creatures under his nailed claws and a salt tear dripping into the river. (He waits for the crashing of glass — alone in our most ultimate distresses we all wait for the crashing of glass when the glittering Redemption will rise, springing corruptible and purified from a pasture of bitterweeds — O endless cycle of suffering that turns between Beast and Prince — and hears only the endless sound of the feet of the bird grinding upon leaves.) Ruin in the peace of after-passion, peaceful and destroyed a little in the ruins of the jack-knife agony, the leaping shrimp-like flexions, in the collapse and debris of earthquake of kiss and trembling, himself a ground ruin, the hiss of finish whispering from the ruin like the aftersmoke over rubble: did he not know that ruin lay wound within the works of everything, for him? That every constructed thing carried hidden in it the intricate greengolden wheels and chains of terror that turned for him? Did he not know that the house of breath and blood that held him promised only terror within every room, where terror would break out through some unconsidered door to chime its own plumed hour of irreversible doom upon him? He walked in the rime of the bog of the icebound bottomlands and heard, with beak of horn and hornéd nails, the bird of fire whose prey he was, chiming his terrible Midnight; his image in the rime of the bog is rainbow . . . . He is Devil, he is Prince, he is Heartbreak. He is destiny of fire, he is ashes and cinders. He is artifice of breath, grinding in his own ruin's cinders under a blown, gray, bubbled moon of breath across a field of ash.

He would come across town and through Bailey's Pasture home to us through the bitterweeds with dock and wild buckwheat in his blonde hair, and below his eyes the blue rims of circles, the color of eggplant, would shine on his flushed cheeks — the Prince of Peace returneth — beast had sprung into Prince in the river-bottoms, agony of vision married to agony of body in the rain, vision eating body, flesh become word. He said — and now I understand — *"Behold this gift of darkness this house has given me and I give you; I have stolen your light away. We are, and never will be. In all your sunshines if you can remember one day any darknesses, that was me drawing you . . . I have left Word in the darkness for you, the Word that was my flesh; all darkness proclaims my Word; listen in the darkness and you will hear it."*

He chose a show to go away with, finally, out of East Texas because I think it was the only bright and glittering thing in the world he could find. Of all the ways and things in the world, he chose a show, with acrobats and lights and spangles. Because he couldn't bear the world without a song and dance and a burnished cane. He was wild like a creature, the way he crept as if he went on paws like an animal out of the brush, a kind of hunted, creeping thing in his gait. He was for the beautiful evil world and he let it ravage him to ash, he gave his life for it. (Was *he* what Christy hunted for in the woods, going with his birdbag and his gun and returning with bird's blood on him and a chatelaine of slain birds girdled round his hips?) He went all the way. He knew what he was and endured it all the way, to the bitter end, burned down to ash by it, charred down to clinker. (I embrace him now, against this wall in the rain.)

They told about the trunks of costumes that came
back to Charity after he took sleeping pills at midnight
in a hotel in San Antonio — they said he was coming
home from New York City and had got that far, lingered
on the very edge of Charity in San Antone but couldn't
come on in home — all the trunks up in the loft, filled
with rhinestones and spangles and boafeathers and
holding the wicked smell of greasepaint. I rummaged
there as if I thought somewhere I might suddenly come
upon some explanation of his mystery.

Brave and noble, Folner? Clean and fine? Boy
Scouts and the Epworth League and all that, Folner?
Pshaw! You didn't want to flicker around East Texas,
you wanted to *blaze* in the world, to sparkle, to shine, to
glisten in the great evil world. You wanted tinsel and
tinfoil and spangle and Roman candle glamor, to be
gaudy and bright as a plaster ruby and a dollar diamond.
Was that right? Of course not. Wrong? What *is* wrong?

"Who has a *choice*, really?" you said.

All of it was wrong from the beginning, from the
corrupted foetus, the poisoned womb, from the galled
cradle (endlessly rocking for you and me, for you and
me).

You were tinsel all the way, beautiful boy Folner, all
the rotten way. Once I said, building a chicken coop, "I
want to make this *right*."

"Nothing is made right around here, Boy," you

said. "Everything is crooked and warped and twisted."

And walked, lost and cheaply grieved, away; and I wondered what you meant.

When your corpse came back to Charity from San Antonio that deep and leaf-haunted autumn, Folner, they embalmed it at Jim Thornton's Funeral Establishment (which was also a cleaning and pressing shop when nobody was dead). There was a gray hearse. All of us went to the Grace Methodist Church and the Starnes and the Ganchions filled up two pews. We sang "Beulah Land" (You would have loved that . . . "for I am drinking from the fountain that never shall run dry (praise God!); I'm feasting on the manna of a bountiful supply . . . "). A few women kept fainting. Aunty sat hating you, even dead. Even laid in a coffin she despised you like a snake. Granny Ganchion sat like a sick bird, humped and bitten, and gazed into your cheap coffin. Oh her hands! — bony and knotted at the knuckles — how she moved them round her goitered throat like a starved woman's. (Do you know what she wore, Folner? A great yellow hat with a boafeather round it, and on her neck was a pair of rubyred beads. What voices were howling round in her head as she sat there, gazing at you in your cheap coffin?) Your brother Christy sat out in front of the church in the car, would not come in, sullen and wretched. As we marched by your coffin to look in at you for the last time, I saw your wasted doll-in-the-rain face and I thought I could hear you whisper to me,

"Make it gay, Boy, make it bright, Boy!" And no one in that whole Grace Methodist Church, or in all of Charity, or in the whole wide world but you and I knew I dropped a little purple spangle into your cheap coffin as I passed by. It was a little purple spangle stolen from a gypsy costume in one of your trunks in the loft. You loved it! It was put in the earth with you.

At your funeral there was a feeling of doom in the Grace Methodist Church, and I sat among my kin feeling dry and throttled in the throat and thought we were all doomed — who are these, who am I, what are we laying away, what splendid, glittering, sinful part of us are we burying like a treasure in the earth?

(The Grace Methodist Church had started out underground. There had been only enough money to build a basement with, and for several years we went down steps into the Church, like a cellar, and had a meeting. In summer it was full of crickets; and often, tired of the singing, we would go outside and sit on the steps and watch the summer toadfrogs leap after and lick in the crickets. But when old Mr. Ralph J. Sanderson, the owner of the sawmill and terror of Negroes, had died, he had left enough money for a ground floor and some colored glass windows and these were added as a memorial to him.)

There were about thirty rows of pews and the Starnes and Ganchions occupied two of them at the funeral. Charity came and filled the rest.

On the raised platform in front under a bare arch were the folding chairs where the choir sat, and to the right of the chairs was the piano. Nina Dot Dooley was the pianist. (She said it peeanist and always ended even the most austere anthem with rolling chords, finishing up on a very high and tinkling treble note with her little finger that was arched over with a dinner ring displayed upon it. She had an orange, spotted face.) In the center of the altar, which was only the barest hint of an altar, stood one spare crooked candle in a goldplated holder: the cause of the schism in the church that finally broke the old and the new factions apart and caused Brother Hildebrandt to form the Church Foursquare and lead his followers with him.

A quartet was sitting straight in the choirloft — it was Mrs. Shanks (called Horseface by all the boys because she had black lips that peeled back off her two rows of large, square, roastingear teeth when she sang out); Miss Pearl Selmers, the alto and the only alto in the church with a trained voice and therefore in every duet or quartet, singing sadly and so faintly you could scarcely hear her; Mr. Bybee, the forced tenor, singing always eeeeeeeee with a quavering sound like a saw played; and Mr. Chuck Addicks, the little old bass.

(Once the Ku Klux Klan interrupted the sermon on Sunday to come marching down the center aisle in their sheets, terrifying the congregation who did not know who among them they might be coming after — but they

had come in only to make a demonstration in favor of the
preacher, of whom they approved, and to give a dona-
tion, wrapped in a white handkerchief, to the church.
One of the sheets moved unevenly with a hobble and
people knew it was Walter Warren Starnes.)

Then the quartet stood, rattling the folding chairs,
and with great austerity sang "For his eye is on the sparrow, and I know he watcheth me . . . ." (You were no
sparrow in that coffin, Folner; you were a plumed and
preened gorgeous bird, hatched in a borrowed nest,
cuckolded, meant for some paradise garden.)

The sermon was a long and sad one. It told about all
the family, about your young life in Charity and your
work in the Church. (Once you had stood, at ten, before
the whole congregation and recited the books of the Bible first forwards, then backwards. You had been a
bright boy. You had sinned. The Lord save your soul.)

I want to make a little speech upon the passing of
this boy, the sermon said. We have lost a leaf from a
beautiful old Charity tree (a leaf! a leaf!). A bright star
has fallen over Charity (a star!). We have lost a jewel (a
sequin! a rhinestone! a parure of great price!), a toy of
the world (O Jack-in-the-Box!). This is a piece of the lavish gay world brought back to Charity black earth, the
bitterweed pollen of the bitterweed of the world clings
to his limbs brought home to this hive. (Green bee that
gyres out of season over us, grown thus into what yield
of bitterweed are we? Pollen to what cilia (spike in the

horses' throat, death in the fowls' craw) of what green
bee of gall?) We are burying the brightness of the world.
We are burying like a foul thing in the dirt this twisted
freak, like Sue Emma's two little monsters, little
slobbering freaks with bloated watermelon heads. Sue
Emma's sins (and every day they'd come and measure
and measure — their head was like Granny Ganchion's
vile goiter, round and swollen and strutted with purple
veins big as a chicken's intestines). O precious shard of
the Old Mother Lode that we bury! Old Mother Lode,
ore of what dark cursed vein?

Songs went through my head, Folner, as I sat there,
songs I had known where, when? "O had I the wings of
Noah's dove, I'd fly away to the one I love . . . ." "One
day you goin come and call my name . . . ." "My love
went away on a long long train . . . ." And the little
verse, piping itself out in my brain, over and over . . . .
"It was just a little doll, dears, brought in from the fields
and the rain; its hair not the least bit curled, dears; and
its arm trodden off by the cows. And its face all melted
away . . . ." And the tale of the gingerbread man who
ran and ran and melted away as he ran . . . . And the
mournful little tune that a child could blow on a petunia;
and the words of the hymn "O Love That Wilt Not Let
Me Go . . . ."

"When I was young," the voices howled round in
Granny Ganchion your mother's head as she sat there
gazing at you in your cheap pink coffin, "I loved gems

and jewels and would almost steal to have a colored ring
to glisten on my finger, just like a Gypsy. We are burying here the glassy part of me. O me . . . . desire fail-
eth; it is the burden of the grasshoppers. *There is a fountain filled with blood, drawn from Immanuel's veins; And
sinners plunged beneath that flood lose all their guilty
stains* . . . . Sure we had nothing in Charity but Beulah
Land to hope for and wait for — but how could that help?
That wasn't enough while we waited. The church
cheated us, Brother Ramsey cheated us. I had to burrow
down *under* it all like a quick mole to have any life. Don't
think I don't know all this. Now there Follie, lay still, lay
still. Remember when I couldn't keep you quiet on a pallet in the summer afternoons when you would have to
take your nap? This is the last pallet, little Follie, a pallet
for good. Lay still on it, child. (There's old Miz Van come
to your funeral — she brought you the first present you
ever got in this world — a pitcher of cold buttermilk the
morning you were born. Fly in the buttermilk Lula
Lula . . . .)

    "What does he say, Brother Ramsey, in his talking,
in his sermon? He is condemning Follie to hellfire. The
Lord hath hung this millstone upon my neck, and I
know what for and I have never told. It is a lavalier of
wickedness. It is the enormous rotten core of Adam's
Apple. But I have had my life in my time — some
way . . . ."

    (You knew lips, how they move to make their

words; and the grimaces of faces when you were yelled at were sometimes so grotesque that you dreamt of them, strained and veined and goggle-eyed — and in your dreams the faces were only making faces at you and not saying anything.

You came to hear only the voices in your head. All the world beyond you was hushed as though some turning of a great wheel was stopped beyond you (but went on inside you), and there remained only the silence of working mouths of shifting faces — and there was only the babel of voices in your head.

When desire failed you, you had nothing left but the betrayal of desire (the moth-eaten coronation robes of dethroned queens) and a pair of ruby beads given you once by a dark alien youth who found you at a carnival and loved you and stayed to love you longer and again. You would steal away at night and run to him at the City Hotel and all the town knew. It was said that Christy was this stranger's son but no one ever proved it, for Christy was black-headed and swarthy among the other towheads — but this could have been the Indian blood that was supposed to be in the Ganchion veins come out in him, you said.

Your father was a southern sea-captain with a wart on the left side of his nose for lechery and by the time you were fourteen he had shot dead two Negroes for not keeping their place and calling him Cap'n.

You had had a hand upon your thigh in the church

choir that made you trill like a meadowlark, "Fling Wide
the Gates!"; and once while singing "Hear The Soft
Whisper" at communion when all the heads were bent,
you received your first baptism of joy — and had been
Joy's sister ever since.)

And then, when the family started walking by your
coffin, Folner, to look at your doll-in-the-rain face for the
last time, Granny Ganchion flung herself into your coffin and tried to seize you to her, crying out in her carline
voice, but you would not come up to her; and they
pulled her away.

As we drove along (what Charity was not in the
procession was standing watching us like a parade) a
storm broke over us and scattered leaves. It was the first
full devastation of Autumn.

We stood around the grave and they let you down
in it while Brother Ramsey sprinkled rose petals. It
seemed he was murmuring, "sawdust to sawdust," and
that surely what was falling was sawdust from the
planing mill. All around the graveyard there was the
ruin of Summer, Summer's wreck and plunder. Weeds
were rusty with seed and the zinnias were crumbling.
And then all the members of the families fell upon each
other, embracing and kissing and wailing and sharing
their separate and secret tragedies; and for a moment at
the Charity Graveyard there was a reunion of blood and
a membership of kin over your grave (the odor of lilies
and carnations gave me a sensuous, exotic elation that I

was ashamed of). There was a kind of meekness and the relief felt in truce. Some took a flower from your grave and fought others to keep it — it was like a battle of fiends over a holy prize; and Aunt Malley came up in a trance and said to Cousin Lottie, "What kin are we all to each other, anyway?"

But the deaf old Mother, wise and bitter and skeptic, did not fall to the graveyard trickery and stood off to herself, gazing at your grave.

There seemed to be some misery over in the world. Some atonement, some ransom was paid for all of us, for all our Sins. Now, in due time and in right season, what resurrection of what spirit would assure us of the meaning of this death, Folner?

As we turned to go away and leave you in the graveyard, I looked back and discovered a tall and sorrowful stranger standing alone by a crepemyrtle tree. It seemed he wanted to say something to me, that he was beckoning to me. But we got in our cars and drove away and he turned and watched us as we went away.

The next day there was a change in the whole world. There was a moon in the daytime like the pale, lashless lid of a drooping eye and it haunted the day. Then rain fell while the sun shone and the devil was beating his wife; birds flew in and over and away, as if bewildered (they knew), one of the hens crowed and a whirlwind got caught in the beantree and rattled the dry pods. I went out among the castorbeans and sat and heard the sad rain, like a faint weeping, dripping on the leaves.

Finally in the afternoon it seemed the whole earth died, dried up and faded and curled. Huge blood-green maple leaves drifted like lost wings in the wind. Hens moulted. Some amputation had happened in the world, some desperate surgery. The fantasy was finished; something crueler was beginning, hard and of agony. The winter was close and lay long and gray and leafless ahead. Something waited for me, now — a world of magic and witchcraft, the brute, haunted world of some nameless terrible beauty, whirling in the twilight glimmer of coming hope and hopelessness. (Who has not seen the gizzard-like birthmark on the luminous temple of the moon?)

Then as the day ended, in the terrifying sunset that was like the ends-of-the-world dusks I had dreaded so often, the rain fell golden in the distance and the golden rain fell over the sawmill, apotheosizing it, as if it had achieved some kind of victory.

You've been buried in Charity for a number of years, Follie, our Follie, and I am called back to the loft where your relics lie stored; and I am here among them rummaging for some answer. It is hard to be in the world and bone of your bone. Cry me out a name, which like a spangle cast out to me, I may carry out of this loft with me.

I come, bending low, into the loft. I had been here once before with Aunty to rummage for a picture of her mother, and when we found the picture it had one eye eaten out by some animal and looked hideous and staring and tormented.

Then I went again and again, with a heavy feeling of sin. I was looking for something *within myself* that might flower out in this warm, secret light, unfurl (I had in my mind the vermilion image of a paper Hallowe'en serpent that would unroll, splendid and quivering, when blown into) like a paper flower dropped in a bowl of water. I felt the excitement — the first I can remember — of discovery, like the feeling I had when I crept into forbidden books. (*Eugenics* was big and black and evil, hidden under the linens of the closet and there I first saw the picture of a woman with a window in her belly through which I could see a little, wound baby, all in a sac entwined by a mass of strings and cords.) I trembled in the loft.

Here in the loft, which is really your sepulchre, Folner, are many things of silence and dignity; and it seems that in them lie all the hope, all the future, in the riot of insects and rodents which are feeding on this storage of antiques.

There is a spinningwheel which spiders have mocked with glittering webs like doilies and lace valentines. There is an organ with a rat world in its insides, and rats' feet sift over the strings with the faintest prism

tinkle like the death-knell of the delicate. On a sugarcane
pole in a corner are strung old dresses and coats and,
crumpled in a corner, is a Ku Klux Klan hood like a
caved-in ghost. The clothes hanging in the purple
loftlight are shredded by claws and streaked by rain and
drenched in light and burned through by ceaseless rays
of sunlight and moonlight and starlight. They are ripped
by teeth and gnawing (almost as if in some kind of ven-
geance) and the tiny punctures of the mouths of ants and
moths, as if the wearing of life had left some sweet syrup
on them. A gray, diaphanous veil hangs like a web and
spun so fine by age that it seems a veil of light. Because
these garments have been so long diffused with light
and lights — through many washings and drenchings —
their colors have faded and the lights have dyed them
delicate pale Light colors.

In an eave is a whole mosque of dirtdobber domes
and gloved hives of bees and the blown gray papier-
mâché bags of wasps. Curtains of gossamer hang
trembling purple and luminous. In this wreckage the
insects and creatures have made their artifice and their
order: frail mouth-built or cilia-built structures, en-
velopes and membranes and spun-out or spat-out fragile architecture, phantom and fantastic and terrifying.

The faded pine walls wear Wear like a fabric, a garment of speared and cometed and darted and spiraled
grain, and grain designs like those on the sole of a foot;
and lacunae of lucent amber resin; and serrated or

glabrous surfaces: a landscape of figures of grotesque naked men and women among pools and hummocks and flumes; and there are fantastic scrawlings and lewd phalliforms of grain. On one wall there is a terrible water-mark figure like the huge claw of an enormous bird grappling over a long dried pool of blood.

There is an old cowboy hat felted with fuzz and fine agglutinated dust.

A pale, watery green sea of Mason jars, and a pile of rubbish onions that had sprouted sickly lianas curling over each other and then withered to crumble are in a dark corner and near them is a croakersack of peanuts, slashed open by some hunger and spilled out like doubloons and now only shriveled husks. And there is a crock, cold to feel, and marbeled like an aged agate.

There stands a churn that has not turned for years.

And behold a group of dolls, limp and dignified, like ancestors sitting together; and some blueing bottles filled with gentian light; and a small tarnished silver key. Away in the farthest end of the loft a big rusted tusk of a plow curves out of the shadow.

The loot of the loft lies like treasure in some thief's lair, and the thief is everywhere so powerfully present I can feel him gathering and fumbling and destroying. Yet all is so silent, except for a tinkling and occasional shiftings like the sound of a page turned in a book.

And then I find the two chests that belonged to you. On the outside is printed GAYETY SHOWS AND

COMPANY. Inside I find out your whole secret.

Inside is a corroded violin whose bow has molded strings furred with raveling, like a rat of hair; some peeling gilded tap-shoes whose taps are thin from much dancing. And false faces, with tragic-gay bent down eyes, women's wigs, tubes of make-up grease, and spangles spilled over the clothes like dried fishscales. And there are fringed gypsy shawls, and scarves, crimson and jacinth and one green as a ragged peacock. I touch a scarf and it falls into air and light and seems to evanesce. And there is a yellow glove and here is a mandarin's lavish emerald-mauve gown with sleeves hanging like pointed asses' ears, with intricate work of golden braid laid tarnished over the hem.

And here is a crushed paper bird on a stick.

Sifted all among the treasures of the chests are letters and photographs of many beautiful played-out people, like lost cards, dealt and used for win or loss and cast away.

At the end of the loft room is an old dresser with a swung mirror. I go there. On the dresser is a pincushion made like a tomato, a mending box full of buttons, a cameo box of beads and cameos and bracelets and balls of faded yarn. Spiders and dust have claimed them all. Next to the dresser is an old ruptured and gutted chair.

"I give you this glass," your voice whispers, "in which to see a vision of yourself, for this is why you've come. My breath is on the glass and you must wipe away my breath to see your own image."

In the mirror I cannot see myself but only an image of dust. I brush it off — and then see my portrait there. For a moment I look like Folner! Within that cornered face, in the purple hollows and fosses of its umbrageous landscape, lie agonies like bruises; this face is thus bruised unreal. But age and time have blown their rheumy breath on the mirror and curdled it and it clouds again. Then I blow my own breath upon the mirror and wipe it clear for another instant. I seem old, I seem unused, as these loft things, in the capture of some thief. The mirror seems to say, "Dance! Swagger with a cane and sequins!"

I cry out, "Folner!" in the loft. But only the rustle of startled creatures and the faint swinging of webs respond.

(I think he ate some kind of bitterweed and suffered a change for the eating and sprang away into a marvelous haunted and haunting world and never could return — although they waited in Charity for him — nor wanted to. Until he was washed (as I am washed against this wall) dead — like uprooted coral weed by some violence only the sea knows and only the sea-depths suffer, upon the oil-rimed and sawdusted shingle of Charity — and was claimed and buried there. They were all looking for him, waiting and watching, and looking for some grass that might take them to him — Granny Ganchion, Berryben, Malley Ganchion, Aunty, Sue

Emma — and even I. And I, having not waited but
wandered for him (calling, "Draw me; I will follow!" but
he murmured, "Whither I go you may not follow me."),
have come back here where I think I might find the
magic he found among the bitterweeds and ate that liberated him and so myself be liberated into under-
standing and cruel authenticity.)

"Love in the cotton gin, my dear. And once, very
early in the delicate watergreen shell of morning, in an
old moored shellbarge on Green's Bayou down around
the Battlegrounds. We got tar on us.

"The C.C.C. Camp at Groveton didn't help. Ah the
East Texas woods in the fall, with flying red leaves like
desires, and the smell of burning brush and that danger-
ous, voluptuous wind of a norther that stabbed the
heart, so evil; like Spanish Fly on the soul . . . Do I
shock you? Of course I say these things, which are
absolutely true, to shock you, you are so good, Boy, you
and Berryben are so damned sweet and good, such
damned sweet kids."

And you dazzled your opal cufflinks at your white
wrists.

"Something cursed me. There was that melancholy
always over me, brooding over me. Why? As far back as I
can remember, lying on the pallet in the summer of the
afternoons, there was the drone of the electric fan, like
the drone of bees, and Mama going through the rooms

in her slip. I felt frail and limp. It was just sorrow bred in me, bred in you too, you'll see; we are the sons of grief at cricket. I had to stop it.

"I was wild for the world of a flashing eye and life castanetting round and stomping an insinuating foot. Sometimes in Charity I couldn't stand it any longer and would go out in the henhouse and make up dreams and play like I was something grand and royal and march up and down with a poker for a cane, with only the chickens to watch me. And then love myself and feel *real* again, a kind of tremor from the world ran through me.

"Behold my talents: Started out in the Church with good Hattie Clegg, led Young People's programs, gave the main speech, sang a solo, then a duet with some girl, then said the final Benediction — it was all my show. Went to Conferences at Lon Morris College, even signed up to be a missionary. I was just looking for some passionate cause in the world to give myself to (so are all of you, all of you) — can I help it if the Church petered out for me? Then I turned to music and the stage. At the high school I was in every play that was put on and I even wrote an original musical show for the Senior Night; and at Grace Methodist Church I was always directing plays, sang in the choir, sang solos, did impersonations on programs in Fellowship Hall, played the piano by ear, anything that was make-believe. To make me forget that cisternwheel turning and turning and that old shuttered house and the family Sundays on the front porch.

"O the drone of the flies and the bees droning in the zinnias like a sound blown by a child on a comb and a piece of tissue-paper; and the melancholy working of the wind in the trees and a whole dead town gleaming out before us in a false serenity under the burning sun of a fleecy summer Sunday sky with a piece of a moon in it, and nothing happening.

"When the circus came to Bailey's Pasture, I knew this was my chance. Remember how you and I and Aunt Malley went and what we saw and did, the yellow-skinned grinning freaks in their stalls with the sawdust floor, twisted like worms the freaks grinned and ground in the sawdust; and the screams of the animals in the menagerie and the sad, exciting music of the calliope? I bought you a paper bird on a stick and here it is, crushed in this loft, to try to tell you something, to try to tell you, even then, that you were lost in Charity and that you had to get away, like me, chiming Charity Cock, to turn in the wind towards the wind's four corners, steeple-cock, welded to Charity churchtops, chanting in the wind. Remember when I lifted you up on that big elephant, you little scared thing perched on that enormous back, you shook and cried and got so excited you almost fainted and Aunt Malley had to run to buy some lemonade and throw it in your face. We were going through the world in Bailey's Pasture that night, my own world, and I wanted to tell you then that I would never see you again and that the world was like this cir-

cus, stall by stall and dazzling Fairies Wheel, and lights
and tights, whirling and gleaming and screaming and
twisting on a sawdust floor. We stood and watched the
birdman clawing his scaly hornéd hands into the sawdust. Then I took you and Malley home and slipped
away again, back to the circus; and met a trapeze man
with thighs in black tights; and stayed and went away
with the circus early that next morning. As we rolled
away in our gay wagons, the last thing I saw of the house
where you lay sleeping was the wheel turning over it,
and the only one in that whole house that I cried for was
you, Boy O Boy.

"In San Antonio I left the circus and took tap
dancing at Hallie Beth Stevens' Studio of the Dance,
sang out in front of a chorus of tapping girls, had a cane
and a hat, and strutted singing, 'You've Got Me in the
Palm of Your Hand' — not before chickens in a Charity
henhouse but a real clapping audience.

"The rest I needn't tell you. Bailey's Pasture was my
revelation.

"They treated me as though I was a freak in Charity,
and I know it was just jealousy and envy. They blamed it
on my mother, your Granny Ganchion, because she
dressed me like a girl when I was little and called me
'Follie.' But it was more than that. Right away I learned
what I was and went on like that, what I was, and *used*
myself for that, made no bones about it — and can't say
the same for most of the rest of Charity who don't know

who they are. What matters if it got me death?

"But if you're going to start calling names, I can tell
you a few things about Brother Ramsey in the church,
who knew me all my life and even preached my funeral
sermon, and who taught me a lot of what I know.
Everything in this world is not black and white, as little
Charity thinks; there are shades in between. And I can
tell some dirt on Jim Lucas and Mimi Day Calkins —
sitting there in the Pastime Club with her finger in his
fly — and Floydell Lucas, his wife, bent over a cradle at
home singing a lullaby — and a lot of other things. (We
are all broken over the cradle, Boy.) Nobody's hands are
clean in Charity. But let Charity flick its old toad's
tongue after the gay green and golden summer flies —
and let them croak away that same old croaking tune.
They don't want anybody to be anything that they can't
understand and give a name to. They had to have some
ready label to lick and stick on you; and when they
couldn't figure me out because I wanted different things
from what they in Charity wanted, they started bullying
me and torturing me. They were all really afraid of me —
and most of them envied me, really envied me.

"The whine and shriek of the planing mill was always in my head, as though they were dressing ship-lap
in my brain. And that hard little mouth of hunger
pressing hot against my soul. To be fed! Who could feed
it in Charity? Oh Charity, I would thou wert cold or hot;
but because thou art lukewarm I will spew thee out!

"I take along some memories. The sight of the black watertower squatting like a fat-bellied reptile over Charity eggs; and the old house smelling of O-Cedar Oil; that old yard of guineas and cackling hens and the manure of cows. But Boy, we had a time of it, didn't we? You little frightened thing, always frightened. On one Easter Sunday I taught you a secret. We rolled away some stone, remember?"

"And you don't know how hard I prayed in the barn in the sunsets I thought were the burning end of the world, Follie. You made me feel so full of sin that I never mentioned your name to anybody; and when once and a while they would say your name I would tremble and think they knew. When the Riverbottom Nigras came to town to tell that they had seen a Haint walking in the sloughs of the riverbottoms I knew it was you come back and at night I lay and watched, trembling on the wall, the shadow of the paper bird made by the fire-light, and I thought I heard its annunciation: *Come away*; and I had nightmares of a haunted bird at night, and never left the kitchen all day, sitting trembling by the woodstove. I thought I heard you at the windows, scratching; and once I am sure I saw you sitting in the Beantree with the three black hens that lived up there. When the preacher spoke about Sin it always had your face. I have just found your real face, Follie my Follie."

"Oh Boy, I had to have some drama in a life. I had a

rhapsody in me. But it devoured me. I was so afraid of what I found out that I began to run and run from it until I melted down into this death. Can you learn anything from this? Tell it — for me; someone has to tell it.

"Somewhere beyond all this muck and dreck there lies a pasture of serenity and I will find it. I am on my way. Hang a wreath on the door of this fallen house for me. How did I die? I invited Death. Because I was so very weary. The rest is a secret never to be told (see seven crows). Leave us alone and we will destroy ourselves in the end, but we will leave undestroyed our other selves to breathe the bridges of breath between our ruined and isolate islands.

"I am the Ur-Follie of many derivations of your time. Find me on walls, most prophetically adumbrated; in shadows of firelight; bursting from clocks; turning on steeples. And I am the beast-muzzled Prince, black-lipped and riverlapping, begging the miracle. Give, and change the Beast. Watch."

"I watch and watch and watch, Follie, and I will build a bridge between these ruined islands; then blow the bridge of breath away. But the islands will remain forever like stone islands in a still and frozen sea. For we are only breath to blow and bridge eternal ruins while we breathe, until we are blown away."

XI

OPEN the cellar door (that swings on hinges of web) and cry down, "Granny Ganchion!" — and rouse the worm called Old Fuzz that the children were always afraid of. Now Granny Ganchion, when you went down in the rootcellar so often I know what happened down here where you sat among all your preserves — the figs and apricots and pears like jewels shining in the Mason jars, shaped like the parts of love. I know you fondled and counted that string of rubyred beads like a rosary.

Here in the cellar, once, when I came down for chowchow, sent by Aunty and trembling to see Old Fuzz, I first discovered where you were when I missed you in the house. I stood at the little cellar door and watched you who couldn't hear me, sitting dressed in a yellow widebrimmed hat with boafeathers round it. I heard, rumbling in the heavens of your world overhead, while you sat down in your Purgatory praying yourself through your beads free of it and into a Paradise of Fruit, the thunder of all their feet in their coming and going, so that their lives must have seemed to you below them only a walking or a rocking; and I know now as you heard their footsteps you named them over, "There's Christy, I can tell the way he walks, he's lookin for me, always tryin to find me; there rocks Malley over me in her rocker by the window, she is rockin across my skull. Goin and comin, backwards and forwards, from gallry to breezeway, they are all walkin and rockin over me and I bend still beneath them here like their dark root in the Charity earth." All your desires were preserved in Mason jars. And then when you saw the light from the cellar door and me standing in it (like what angel come in light through your door?) you jumped and made your *uck uck* sounds and then murmured, "Boy! Boy!" as though I was a lover called to you by your wishing for him and you were waiting, ready for him. And then I closed the door. They said I was pale when I came back without the chowchow and that it was because I had seen Old Fuzz in the cellar, and laughed and ate without it.

But what I saw was the truth of you, Granny Ganchion, that I know now and now give back to you in this cellar, and leave it here. I know you sat down here with Old Fuzz, that I always imagined to be like some great green-warted worm coiled down here, and that he said to you, "Hannah Ganchion, you got nothin in the

world but a few hundred jars of rotten preserves and an
old pair of rubyred beads. The rest is silence and no love
and no brightness anywhere, only a house full of silent
folks makin faces at you. And an old dead husband,
Gentry Ganchion, that used to say to you, 'All right,
Hannah, then I swear to God I'll go downtown to the
City Hotel!' " (and the time I heard the whores in the city
jail, blessed damozels leaning their heads out the golden
windows singing, "Bless them all, bless them all, the
long and the short and the tall") "and him sneakin over
to niggertown right from your own bed at midnight,
while ever month there was a nigger tarred and feath-
ered and beaten up on Rob Hill because he'd raped an
East Texis white woman" (they said you weren't a man
in East Texas until you'd had a nigger woman); " and
you just finally drove him away and he went to St. Louis
and died, alone, in a convalescent Home."

"And you protested to Old Fuzz that you had
Christy and that you had had Folner and that you had
had a time in your own time. And then the worm flashed
and said, "That's a lie and a fairytale! You know it and
the preserves know it the the rubyred beads know it.
You know Folner's done strange things like goin away
with a show and everyone says there was something
wrong with him — the time he came home in patent
leather shoes and even had a permanent wave in his
blonde hair proved it. And what happened around
Charity and the commotion he caused among the young

boys, and everyone sayin he acted just like a girl — and at the depot when they took his used-up, burnt-out body off the train, people of Charity saw box after box of costumes with spangles and rhineṣtones and boafeathers and said, lookin in, "Can this be all that's left of Folner Ganchion to come back from San Antone: spangles and rhinestones and boafeathers?' "

But you said, "Them was all lies in a little town. Cause they come home, Christy come home and Follie come home . . . . O my sons and daughters . . . ! Wrenched screamin out of me and I couldn't even hear their screams . . . !

"Worm! Where did I come from, who was I . . . . I cain't remember . . . ."

"You was born and raised in Alabama, ran with a flock of children through the pastures like geese; and your papa was a sea captain besides ownin about a dozen Negroes that worked his cottonfields . . . ."

"I remember, I remember . . . . Worm! How did I ever meet Gentry Ganchion, that ole cuss that finally went off to Saint Louis and died there? Tell me . . . ."

"He wasn't the first you met, nor the last. Tell yusself. That's why you come down here. Tell yusself."

"Deafness is hearin just a person's own voice; who's deaf to their own voice? But it seems like I'm talkin to somebody hearin me. Somebody settin someplace thinkin of all their life . . . . What does that mean? Thinkin how their life, now that it is near the end of their

life, and all lives, uz like some book read, with some plot
and story to it, and things happenin in it to make a long
and unbelievable story — would anybody ever believe it
if I told it? — and how now they knew what their life as a
story had been, just in one moment settin somewhere in
a moment of clearin they see it clear and what was all in
it, all along the line. So that they could tell it, after that —
to who? To theirselves is enough — like a made-up
story, or sing it out like somebody in a Christmas can-
tata, comin in suddenly where there are people gathered
round and singin out the long long story of what had
happened to them in their experience. And that this was
it: how a person could come to them (that was Vester
Langley) and in a orchard (this was Hare's orchard) under flowers on boughs and under petals of broken flowers on the spring grass, and where there was danger of
bein caught, and how for the first time in their lives they
were touched and give up and let it happen. And then —
uck uck — how a warmth like a ray of sun slipped in
them, havin no shape or weight it seemed: quiverin,
brilliant, feelin like a golden minnow or a goldfish and
felt to them like the feel of a minnow slippin through the
hand; and then it lept and jerked and jackknifed like a
leapin fish. And how, lyin under what could be in the
summer fruit hangin on the fruittrees, they could, then,
they learnt in that orchard, be sworded by a sword of
warmth, be bladed by some blade, and set aglow like a
Fourth a July night by this.

"And then how they could go along (this was still Vester) and this happen here and that happen there, making things worst or making things better, and in the orchard pears hung low and heavy and they touched them and loved them in their hands and then how they laid under the peartrees with the pears in their faces.

"Oh there could be the pears that I put up, brought by by Mr. Hare. And those plums, they could be the blossoms I putt in my hair and that I laid under and had fallin on my face (before it slid down like icin on a cake into this fallen face), that I laid on. Mind as well see that things come round to an end if you wait long enough. Look look at the fruit!" (I see the fruit in their jars like ruined aquariums with their corpses of fishes: rhubarb, indigo plums, green cherries, and once golden apricots; the wizened sapless figs.)

"And then how at the end a summer Vester went off to the North and I was left alone. And how I waited and waited until another one came, and this was Jeff Cranberry and how I married him and how we went along, not too good, until he was shot in the buggy with me settin by him. I had a baby comin and that was Lauralee. Then the whole town made a fuss over me because I was a widow and a pretty one, and one who made a fuss was Gentry Ganchion and we married. Had Malley right away. Then nothin but sawmills forever after, I married sawdust. Then we come to Texis to the Charity Sawmill. The noon whistle and Gentry comin

home for dinner. But in some year, when it twas I don't
know now, the Carnival come, and I spun a wheel and
he knocked niggerbabies down to win these beads — he
wanted to brush the sawdust that we had laid in off my
skirt but I said let it be you'll *never* brush that sawdust
off.

"Then Christy come. When Christy was made in
me his maker made him in sorrow and tears in a wet tent
and on sawdust, and we cried together; O Lord that face!
Bobblin and swimmin over me, that face before my face
starin down on my face pressin against my face, with
such sadness in it, eyes closed, eyes wild as storm
moons, teeth grittin and mouth hot and pantin — over
my face this face, ghost-faced, until it closed down upon
me and fitted upon me like a mask and our faces melted
into each other, his tongue slippin into my mouth, ready
mouth, and our faces meltin into each other . . . Then
all down the line and length of us we fitted and melted
and mixed, swellin into hollow, knowin we uz made for
this, like tongue n groove . . . . And I rocked him in the
cradle of myself . . . .

"He was divin, divin, down down — and risin —
and fallin — and then when we touched everwhere, and
locked tight and rocked like one person so that we felt
like one tiny cog, oiled, turnin smoothly and without
one sound the whole, huge cisternwheel of the human
race — it happened up inside us, and we cried; and
broke apart; and saw through the splits in the tent the

burstin flashes of the whirlimagig and heard again the
music of the hobbyhorses like a frenchharp.

"And then we went out and threw baseballs at
niggerbabies and he won me this pair of beads.

"But when Follie was made, Gentry laughed (he always laughed) and bleated like a wild goat. How I
despised that goatlaugh; and finally I couldn't hear it
and I thanked the Lord I'uz deaf.

"O I've held, bent over in me, like in some sorrow,
the folded childrun in me; I've held in me, like a capsule,
a little world, the germ of all that can happen to anybody, carried little worlds round in me round as a globe,
and I thrust worlds out into the world. I've held these
breaths breathed into me, and the man that touched
these breaths and brought em up from the cellar of my
womb out of me was Dr. Currie Monette. And I know
what happened when he touched the breath in me and
brought it up from me, this breath was brought up in joy
and I shuddered and sank away into my sleep.

"I have seen Roma the cow come home from the
pasture over the rayroad tracks and through the gate,
home to the fold. Her milk was the milk of bitterweeds
and through my breasts (like dog's ears now) and
through the breasts of my daughters Malley and
Lauralee the bittermilk was passed on to childrun of this
house. I've seen the folks of this house come back from
places they'd gone to, while I set here through the years,
Christy from his Merchant Marines and Follie in a

casket. I've seen the river come over the pasture, too . . .

"All I need do is touch a bead — and although I cain't feel joy now I can sure remember what it *felt* like to feel joy when I could feel it. Oh I've had my life in my time and out of it, such a fertilized field, I've bred my childrun of Joy. Now the caterpillar is on the leaf, the mildew upon the stalk and the worm is in the bud. When you get old and everthing goes from you and all your childrun go from you, you are shut off from everthing, you have only Ole Fuzz that you used to scare all the childrun with left that scares you now, that still lives on in the delapidated, cold and decrepid nest. The life of all olefolks is just a shambles of the nest where the moulty old worm sets, in a pest of all the lice of memry — built of birds' spit and spiders' hair and ole women's gray hairs — the nest is withered and fallin away. We mothers kicked a crooked cradle and it rocks forever and ever like a dry nest in a leafless dead tree.

"But O we cure ourselves, we do it with ourselves and by ourselves, we are our own cure and nobody else. We're sick and then get well again and then are sick all over. Sometimes I think women are nothin but womb-tumors and blood and afterbirth; but they get well and clean again and then they take on all their sickness through more joy: in the sickness lies the cure.

"Ole Fuzz, you and I have loved this souring fruit — your scales are Follie's spangles, your warts are my goiter; wens, chancres and shale cover your body. Sometimes I believe you breathed out this house from your dragon nostrils. Sometimes I think *you* are the worm in that fruit, that *you* are the caterpillar on the leaf. Ole Fuzz, this house blown down into these ruins is built of feathers and shells and webs and spangles and beads; and sometimes I think that if you'd blow hard you could blow it all away, and that after a minute's noise of somethin soundin like the breeze in a prism-curtain, there'd be no more house and jest silence forevermore.

"This house was putt together from the inside like Christy's ship in the bottle and like the sea in Swimma's seashell — somethin put us all inside it, like that haunted somethin that someway putt the breath of the sea in the shell or our own breath into us. Seems like I've got the memry of the whole race of people in me — somethin returned to everthing; somethin always comes back . . . *wait for the comin back;* the years go and the years come back and it never ends, with us all in all of them, goin on as everthing that ever was, changin one into another, mothers and sons. I may be deaf, Ole Fuzz, but I know this; and I can hear a bucket splashed in the well and I can hear the grindin of the cisternwheel and I know I'll carry the whine of the planin mill inside my head until I die, and probly foreverafter . . .

"Now tell me worm, where did I come from, cain't remember . . . "

"Tell yusself . . . "

"I touch the beads for Christy . . . "

XII

WHAT WAS this man with a long houndface and a glistening silver eye who tacked this map to the kitchen wall and gazed and gazed at it? (How old and worn the world looks now! From too much gazing Christy faded the world like too much light on colors; he has taken the luster into himself and looked the luster into me, stamped it upon my skull so that my skull became a globe of the world.) His image is teardrops of birds' blood speckled on his denimed thigh, a waist girdled by a wreath of small dead birds, and axewound's scar secret on my thigh. And about his image there resounds an echo of frenchharp music and of clashing beaks of horn.

Christy was big and had dark wrong blood and a glistening beard, the bones in his russet Indian cheeks were thick and arched high and they curved round the deep eye-cavities where two great silver eyes shaped like bird's eggs were set in deep — half-closed eyes

furred round by grilled lashes that laced together and
locked over his eyes.

He was a hunting man; and hunted; and his mother
Granny Ganchion was a shaggy old falcon that had
caught him like a surrendered bird and held him close to
her, home; as though he had been hunted in his own
hunting, the hunter hunted; and captured: by trap or
talon; or treed; or set or pointed at and stalked in his own
secret woods and brought home, driven towards stall
and what forage, at nightfall, to her, the hunter's hunt-
ress. He had had one friend before me, he said, and that
was his mother (O cries into a deaf world!) who could
not hear him, only read off his lips his passion that lay so
fair and lovely, trembling on his full wiener-colored
lips. He had just talked so long into deafness that he
came to judge the whole world deaf, and so he no longer
said anything much (could or would he be heard?). It
was what he didn't say that said what he said (I think I
know now what he didn't say). He became a man of ges-
tures: shrugging his humped shoulders under his work-
shirt like a big bag carried there; waving his long
scarecrow arms with raveled strips of fingers, long-
nailed and hanging down at the end of his arms like the
raveling out of arms (the isinglass nails shaped like oval
shells were bent over sharp and tough at the ends as
roosters' spurs are); throwing his great dark head from
side to side or tossing it up and down in horse move-
ments; and, in his despairs, heaving up in the air the

whole huge, buoyant, winged upper portion of his
body, arms and bladed torso, like enormous agitating
wings of a huge and sinewed man-angel.

Christy made everything seem an evil secret — the
songs he sang to his guitar: "Write me a letter, send it by
mail; send it in care of Birmingham Jail . . . ," and he
would be in jail singing this song because he had done
something wrong in the woods or with the Mexicans.
He had a circumcision-like scar, pink and folded, on his
brown neck over which he would gently rub his fingers
and tell me how it was a knifecut because of love. When
Christy yodeled, flashing his silver eye, "You get a line,
I'll get a pole; we'll go fishin in a crawdad hole, Ba-abe,"
he was telling me long, long stories of woods-meetings.
He would go off hunting (in Folner's same woods), leaving me behind and wondering ("One day when you're
old enough I'll take you huntin with me, we'll go huntin,
Boy") and then come back to us as though he had been in
some sorrow in the woods, with birds' blood on him and
a bouquet of small, wilted doves hanging from his waist
over his thigh, or a wreath of shot creatures: small birds
with rainbowed necks, a squirrel with a broken mouth
of agony. Then he would come to me and speak, for he
had found words, "Listen Boy, listen; come out to the
woodshed with me quick and let me show you somethin, come with me, quick; by Gum I've got somethin . . . "

What would he show me if I went?

They said around Charity that he did the thing that
would make you crazy if you did it too much; they said
he was a niggerlover; they said he was a KuKlux; they
said he was adopted by Granny Ganchion and was a no-
good Peepin Tom whose parents were probably foreign-
ers or Jews or thieves in the Pen; and some of this was
true and he was bad. But after he dived down into the
river and found Otey, his wife, and brought her up to
the shore, drowned, he was a different man.

He hated Folner, said he had to squat to pee and
didn't have enough sense to pour it out of a boot. He had
raised him like a mother ("Folner came when I was
fourteen and Mama was sick, sick before he came (the
way I knew he was comin was when I asked Mama if she
had a pillow stuffed there and she said, 'No, it's going to
be a little baby'), sick to almost dyin when he was born
(and had to have him Cicerian, Follie came out her side,
came into this world sideways), and sick always afterwards. I was Follie's mother all those years, makes me
part woman and I know it and I'll never get over it. How I
rocked him and how I slept warm with him at nights,
rolled up against my stomach and how I never left him
day nor night, bless his little soul, settin on the gallry
with him on my knee while I watched the others comin
and goin across the pasture to town and back from town,
to Chatauquas and May Fetes. Until he changed. What
was it got hold of him? Took to swingin in the gallry
swing all day, by hisself, turned away from me, some-

thin wild got in his eye, and then Mama took him back. Began to wear Mama's kimona and highheeled shoes and play show, dancin out from behind a sheet for a curtain; and then I turned away from him . . . Oh what does it mean tellin and rememberin all this — except that it has made me what I am right now: somebody settin here tellin and rememberin what made them what they are right now . . . "); he had raised him like a mother until Folner turned away from him and hated him, and then Christy said he was a sissy and a maphrodite (but they joined again in the woods — where I joined them too; and now we all join in the world).

He would say whispered things about animals: udders, the swinging sex of horses, the maneuvers of cocks, bulls' ballocks and fresh sheep — he was in some secret conspiracy with all animals. He fought game and Cornish cocks with the Gypsies and the Mexicans, and often he would clink in his hand some dangerous-looking tin cockspurs that he used for his fighting roosters. But after a roosterfight with the Mexicans or a hunt in the woods, Christy would be quiet and then sit all day close to Granny whittling little figures; and once he carved a perfect ship and put it in a bottle.

Out in the woodshed Christy played a frenchharp cuddled in his trembling hands, blowing and sucking sounds like birdcalls and moaning voices of animals; and before I knew him I lay in my bed hearing these sounds like a mystic music played from the moon that rocked like an azure boat in our sky, framed by my window. Everything Christy never said was whispered, lipped, blown into his frenchharp; and his pale wet lips curled like some delicious membrane; or like the workings of fishes' mouths that might be saying something under water.

He had had a little wife named Otey and they had lived sometime together in a shack up the road beyond the house; then they both went home again, she to her folks at Clodeen and he back to Granny Ganchion. Otey had big daisy eyes, yellow with lashes like sun rays radiating from the hazel centers; and a sunlight shone from them. But her hands were long and frail and purplish, shaped like frogfeet, with tiny white bones white under the skin. O her frail frogfeet hands holding a bouquet of Cups and Saucers brought from the fields to Granny Ganchion! (who always sneezed immediately). (Granny would say, "Christy what's the matter with Otey, she's as white as a pile of chalk; pore as a snake."

"She's just tarred, Mama," Christy would say.

"She's such a sunk-in little thing, all bowed over. I don't see how she's worth much at her chores, that Otey's sick, Christy, her skin's real crepey.")

They would come down the sandy road, Christy deep in his silence, Otey's bare feet glad in the cool yellow sand of the old wagon road, coming bent over, and good, down the road to the house. Christy would say,

"Otey we got to go and be with Mama, Mama's lonesome." Then they would come down to us and Christy and Granny'd just sit, not saying a word much, Granny uttering her *uck uck* sounds because of her goiter, that sounded like an old setting hen safe with her eggs.

Sometimes if they didn't come, Granny would say, "Why don't Christy come down to see me; why don't none of my children ever come to see me?"

And then she would send me up the road after Christy. I would find him sitting on their little porch, huge and quiet, and Otey no place to be found. Then Christy would call into the trees for her, sounding her name through all the woods; and finally she would come, very softly and bent over from the trees, holding some wood she had gathered. "We got to go down to the house, Otey," he'd say. "Mama wants us."

I know that while he sat on the little porch of his shack in the woods, voices called to him, "Come home, come home," and that the doves moaned this and the owls hooted it, "Come home, come home"; and that I must have seemed to him like another bird when I came to him from the house calling, "They want you home."

Then once, in the hottest summertime, he came to me and whispered to meet him in the woods to catch a mother possum and her babies. I trembled to go, and slipped away and met him. I saw him waiting for me (like a lover), I saw him sitting on a stump watching me as I came, closer and closer, feeling evil, feeling guilty.

We rejoiced (without words) at our meeting secretly.

The mother possum lived in the rotten stump on an old tree, and when we found it Christy began chopping at it with an axe. Because I came too close to him once he came down on my thigh with his axe — so gently that he only cut a purple line under the skin and no blood came. I almost fainted and fell to the ground but did not cry. But Christy wept and begged me not to tell anyone and tied his bandanna tightly round the wound and hugged me and trembled; and I have never told. I have carried on my thigh the secret scar he left me (O see the wound on this thigh left by that hunter's hand!) and have never told.

But we got the little possums and put them in a chicken coop at night. The next morning they were gone — as if they had never been there and we had only caught them in a dream of mine; yet I saw the purple axewound on my thigh and found a hole scratched out under the chicken coop, and so I knew it really happened, and that no one but Christy and I would ever know.

After that, there was a long time of waiting in which I knew there was a preparation for something. Within this waiting (was Christy waiting too?) we looked at the map together or I watched him make the ship in the bottle or heard the frenchharp in the woodshed.

And then one summer night I learned his truth (and

mine). It was through a window that I learned it when, wondering what he was, I squatted in the garden ducking down under the peavines, outside his room, and watched him through leaves of moonlit vines. It seemed he was floating above me and that I was seeing him through thin-shaled waving leaf and light patterns of water; and the light through the tiny bones of waving leaves made him have green feathery lines winnowing over his body and he was spotted and speckled with dark leafshapes, marked like a fish. From where I watched him from below it seemed he might at some moment dive down to me and embrace me and there speak and say, "Listen Boy, listen, let me tell you something . . . " There, in the garden, I, like Eve, found him leaf-shadowed (and, like Eve, leaf would forever after make me stop to remember). There he lay, among vines now, so beautiful in his naked sleep, and so stilled (I thought) — a hot liquid summer night filling the world with the odor of greengrowing and moonlight — green-golden under the light he had fallen asleep with still on, little cupids of gnats wafting round him. I found him hairy with a dark down, and nippled, and shafted in an ominous place that I seemed to have so known about always in my memory, not new, although suddenly like a discovery, that I whispered to myself "Yes!" — as though I was affirming forever something I had always guessed was true. He lay among the vines decorated with a stalked flower — or was it a flame licking up out of him — so quiet, yet with some inner commotion going on within him, perhaps a dream he was having of being discovered like this, all gentle and in his prime and bloom: he lay blooming among the vines, in my moonlight; and in all this soft night I had him before me, eternal shape of man, all my own discovered resplendent prize in the world, caught unfolded like a flowerless daytime plant into its unsurmised nightflower by the wild eye of a little animal, glorious in his solitary unsuspected blessing (yet somehow always known about — we all know, how?) and diving in his dream of quest for something to pull to him and embrace in some glory, through some power that would create him *man*, defined, real, continuing man in me, through the window. Snakes, I thought, slough, under ferns, in their time, and what eye sees them? Shells open at their tide and moon on shores where only moon sees and tide knows: I am something old and mysterious and wise as moon and tide; for I have seen; and I will never tell but *be* what I see here, in my time. O what was it in the life of things that prized open the shells, lifted up the bloom off stalks, and slipped the skin off serpents, on and on and on?

Then I climbed up in the chinaberry tree and looked at him again and it seemed he was lying in the branches, bough in bloom or fruit on a tree.

After that I knew how beautiful he could be, that he had his beauty cursed or blessed, as though it was

smitten, on him, close as flesh; and when I later saw all
adornments of bodies and of the world: spires of ancient
churches where birds lived among bells as though the
birds were flown-out bells ringing in the sky; light
through stained glass Creations of naked Adams on
windows (and Adams expulsed, with hands like leaves
covering their flower that, in another garden, had
caused all Christy's woe), signs seen on boughs and
bodies, flowers and gems and flames; stars, eyes: the
torment of their luster; the infinite fairness of veined
temples, stretched hands like wings of birds — I recalled
him that I saw like my creation of man, through a window, floating and flowering in my early moonlit
darkness among the peavines and the boughs of the
chinaberry tree — and thought that this vision must be
the meaning of boy beholden to man.

I went out in the road and walked in the moonlit
sand and thought, *O when I am ready, really ready, and
filled with blood, I will go, before I die and in my strength,
hung with my beauty blooming close upon my flesh and this
vision burned upon my brain, in the spring, through all the
land, sowing it with my substance, lying under fruittrees in
meadows and on hills with all the young; and brush the leaf
away. And we will fill the world with our sighs of yes! and
make it sensual like rain, like sun, like scents on wind, being
blossoms and pollen: flowing and flying coupled over the
world and sowing our wealth into it, fertilizing it. My life
will be for making the world an orchard.*

And then, finally, it was the time Christy had whispered about. We rose early and went away into the woods in a blue, wet world to hunt together. The sky was streaked like broken agate, as if the huge bowl were porcelain or agate and had been cracked; and it seemed there were no clouds anywhere in the world. Christy and I were sleepwalkers going away from a house of breath and dream. The sound of a chopping axe echoed in the acoustics of the agate heavens. I was so afraid; we were going, it seemed, towards some terrible mission in the woods. The sad, dirty face of Clegg's house looked at us as we passed it.

A fragile, melodious Oriental language blew in on the wind like the odor of a flower and we saw the string of smoke from a gypsy camp somewhere in the woods. The sliding of our feet in the road flushed a flutter of wings from the bush. The fields were alive with things rushing and running; winged and legged things were going where they would, no engine or human to stop them. Out in the fields under the thick brush and in the grass and green were myriad unseen small things that were running or resting from running. Under the trees as we went we swept back the webs and broke them as we went. What was this terrifying rising of something in me, like a rising of fluid? Some wild and mourning thing was calling and claiming me. It was autumn and the time of the killing of hogs; there were squeals in the distance. Dandelions whirled like worlds of light. Hickory nuts were falling. Folner lay buried in the graveyard; and Otey, too. We only looked that way, toward the graves, as we passed, and carried their lives within us as we went towards the woods.

We climbed a little hill and he stood for a moment on the hill, all his life breaking with loneliness and memory inside him, looking down on the country of Charity behind and the river ahead like the wolf in the picture in Aunty's room. As we came down the hill on the river's side we were walking down the slopes of the strangest, yellowest world to a wide field that seemed the color of a pheasant's wing. And then a bird appeared. Instantaneously Christy shot it dead. He picked it up and we went on. We passed the carious ruins of an old shed. Two Negro women appeared from behind it. "Blackbirds!" some voice said. "We can watch them wash in the river (ever seen a nigger's tits? Big as coconuts . . .)." But we went on. And then we came into the bottomlands where the palmettos were turning yellow. At the river, which seemed to have just waked and was clucking in its cradle, we saw the leaves falling into the river. Now not a living creature ran or rustled. There was only the occasional comma of dropped cones punctuating the long flowing syntax of the river's sentence. Then the river bent and we followed it, and there the river was drugged in the early morning and creeping so slowly that where many leaves had fallen and gathered the river seemed a river of leaves.

These were Folner's woods. What had he found here or left? Once we saw, in the sand, the prints of knees left by someone who had kneeled and drunk from the river; and then I saw Christy get down on his hands and knees and drink like a beast from the river, and I saw the signs his body left there.

We walked along under the ragged trees and pieces of them were forever falling falling about us as we went; as though the world was raveling into pieces and falling upon us as we went, Christy ahead, silent and huge under his hunting cap, his isinglass nails shining, and I behind, afraid and enchanted. No fishes were making the noise a rock makes dropped in the water; only a watermoccasin, once, was skiffing along soundlessly with his brown head erect like the head of an arrow. We were going through the ruin and falling away of dreams, Christy and I — come from the house filled with its voices, going towards our reality that, once found and taken, would fall away again into dream.

And then a purring, gurgling sound came as if it were the river; but it was Christy's frenchharp.

We passed a muscadine vine with grapes that had some silvery frenchharp music's breath blown on them. There was the sound of the hopping of birds on leaves.

And then Christy suddenly shot at a turtle that looked like a rock, and got him.

He shot again and a dove fell, followed by the falling blessing of feathers. He looked at me, asking me to pick up the fallen dove. I picked it up, ruined. We went on.

We were going after all marvelous things; silently; he going ahead blowing and sucking his frenchharp; I behind, timid, and terrified and marching in an enchantment by the music in the woods. For a time he was leading me like a piper to the river; and for a time I was following in a kind of glory, and eager, and surrendered, and wanting to follow — just as he was, in his own dumb sorcery and splendor, leading me, victor, proud, like a captive. But the uncaptured, unhypnotized part of me was afraid, wanting to run home (where was home to run to, towards where?); for I knew he was leading me to a terrible dialogue in the deepest woods. All his hunting, all his shooting and gathering up of shot birds was a preparation — like a meditation in which there is a collection of words, for prayer or protestation or farewell or betrayal — in which he would tell me some terrible secret. In it he would finally, after making me wait until I was almost mad with desire for words from him, tell me all the Evil and arm me for all the Joy that there could be and be had, in the world; and I would have no one to tell it to, to contain it, just as he had had no one, only the hunt and this boy. But until the moment of speech in the deepest shadowed woods where it seemed we would be in a cistern, let down alone together for this terrible revelation of secrets, Christy's silence was the ringing starry soundlessness of night in the woods, of deafness got from his mother. (I carried his news for years within me until now I tell it. Evil comes free to you, it had been purchased for you as a gift. But steal Joy, he told me, find and rob it out of the world, suffer for it but steal Joy like a thief of despair.) ("Yet that's what Folner did and you despised him," I would answer him if we could have a conversation now — O Christy, if you were here! We could have a conversation.) Now the river flowed like his own wordless speech.

We looked across the river toward the ahead — long flat brown land — and we wanted separately and silently to start across the field away toward something ahead. He said to me fly away from here — I give you these bird's wings to fly away with from here where we are all just the sawed-off ends of old tubafours rottin on a sawdust heap; fly up and away, across the river past Riverside and on away. And what brings you down will be what gave you wings to fly up and away, will be what needs to use you to speak with; be bird, be word. (Yet as we went, "come home, come ho-o-me," the voices called. The doves moaned this and the owls hooted it, "come home, come ho-o-me, . . . ")

"But when I would run home, what would there be for me to do? Only set by Mama while she rocked and hear her go uck uck in her throat and watch the goiter sliding up and down under her lank skin, rising and falling. But in the woods I had my life – and in some other places.

"Towards the river – across! The birds! What went by?

Wings! O wing me over! Come over, come over, let Christy come over! Hell-o! Hell-ooo! Listen to the echo O-O-O! suffering from the other side. But Boy, we'll send you over. When he runs to me, bringing a bird, it is Freshness, Newness, Unusedness running to me — O come to me! Let me touch your untouched newness (I am old and cold, but burning). Let me shoot you like a shining cartridge over the river and into the fields of the world.

"To swim like a fish up the river to the mouth, O Great Mouth to swallow me in, home to the end. O my blue face! That I bite my fingernails — that they will know and say I'm crazy — the time I dove in the river and goin down what happened and comin up how it happened, comin comin — Oh God Almighty I'd do it twenty times a day, to shudder like that, to forget, shuddering like that, everything but what is lovely and warm and nothin. And then how I sat down dizzy on the banks and wept, on the banks of the river I cried — by the waters of the Charity I sat down and wept. O Otey I had you at last, I had you, caught in my hands, alone and wrapped together in the soft crepedesheen cloths of the waters of Charity I had you, nekkid I had you, below the surface of the river, where above they all sat waitin for us; and when we came up to the top and the light and world you were dead and I was deaf and dumb and blind. They laid us both on the shore and one of us never did come to, and that was you.

"But now let us go — we are going after it, what we never had. If it lies across the river, I cannot cross the River. O Bird! Wing me over the River! This young

brightness following me will one day cross the River for
all of us, we will send him over. I will tell him to go, by
killing the next bird I will tell him to — there's the wing
of a dove, sounds like a flying frenchharp . . . Got it, by
gum, look at the falling wings, look, look at the falling
wings! Let Boy run to get it like any birddog. Hey,
young sad birddog, Hey, Birddog! He is fresh to be
used, this cleanpeckered boy, keep him away from the
niggers and the cows, keep him away from himself,
keep him from the fruits like Follie, my own brother.
There's another beak — it's a woodpecker — tell him by
the stopping of a woodpecker's pecker — Zing! got him,
by gum (Hey, Birddog!).

"To wash out my mind of all these remembrances
— who can I tell them to, to get rid of them? Boy will listen, he is just nothin but a little quiet listener, I'll tell
him, tell him with words when the moment comes. It
will be in the thicket and he will be waitin for it, he is always waitin to hear. Children are the ones to tell things
to, they are the only keepers of secrets in the world. I'll
tell Boy (Hey, Birddog!).

"I remember an Owal. I remember a blue Owal in a
cave by the bend of this river. I saw him at twilight as we
were headin home from our huntin trip, Walter Warren,
Ollie Cheatham and myself (the men coughin in the
tents at night; the sad dyin fire dyin down in the cold;
the night with stars caught in my mosquitobar up over
me, and me cold upon the ground hearin only a call of

some animal off somewhere, a stream runnin on, the
coughin of Walter Warren and Ollie, and the chokin of
the fire. In the smells I smelt was a whole world that
could never *be,* only be breathed in and make in me
pinecones and windscents and earth — someone to be
this smelt world with, be still with me! to be calm with!
someone to be still in!); first, I *felt* somethin in that
grotto, then I looked and it was the blue Owal. I never
told anyone, but I knew there was an Owal in there. I've
remembered that Owal for years, for fifteen years that
Owal's been in the cave of my memory, settin there blue
and still. What does anything settin like that mean?
What does Mama mean, settin there in that house? In
that cellar? There's a meanin! There's a meanin! One
time we stood on a hill and looked down at the crawlin
river below. There were animals down there, I don't
know what kind, couldn't make em out, but I could *feel*
animals down there. There was a huge moon about to
bust in the sky. Suddenly lookin down there, with the
moon heavy over me and the animals movin around
below, I felt somethin that had been like this before, way
back somewhere, the way you do, you know, the same
kind of feelin — it was in Deridder Loosiana, when we
was all there and kids, and Papa was travelin for the rayroad; and one night in my room I was waked up by the
feelin of the sky pressin down on me, and of somethin
movin, some life of some kind rustlin around me, and I
went to the winda and looked out to see this big lop-

sided moon about to bust in the sky and across in the
next house I saw a bare arm reach out from a bed and
slowly pull down the shade. As the shade was comin
down I saw legs wound around in some kind of fightin;
and then the light went out. I squatted there and
couldn't hear nothin, couldn't see nothin, but I knew
there was some commotion of life goin on in there in that
blinded room, I could *feel* it. (There's a meanin! There's a
meanin!) (I had seen insects coupled in flight; and this
was like that, insect legs locked, and there was a kind of
huge flight, of enormous but ever-so-light leapin, and
beatin of a kind of wings: a risin and a flutterin and a
fallin. Then I thought how two can be caught in some
crisis that they seem to be desperately tryin to get out of
together, strugglin to help each other yet each wrestlin
to get somethin the other has and wants to give up but is
waitin to give it up just a little longer, *won't* give it up (O
when . . . Hurry hurry . . .), and in which there is
pain; and wordlessness; and tears. For I knew, even
then, that we all have got somethin in us that will give
pain, that will make somebody go *uhuh uhuh uhuh* and
wag's tongue and roll's eyes and breathe as though he is
gaspin or suffocatin with the croup, or say *whew! whew!*
as though he is burnt; and almost die. To give this pain,
and to get it, we will do almost anything. All those years
I would do anything, anything to get this pain — but
then it got to where the pain I wanted could not be
reached by any hands, it moved down so far inside me

that nothin could reach it. Oh Lord, from all that hap-
pens to anybody in this world you'd think they'd never
want to live . . .) And then I knew that there was a fight
goin on in the world — for things I dreamt of but never
thought you could get, but so wanted, so wanted. And
then O I wanted to holler out because I was so clost to
bustin like the moon, because I was so lonesome and so
lonesome, and there was nothin I could do, bein
eighteen, because I so wanted legs wound around me
and to fight and to be pressed down on, hot and soft, but
do the thing that will make you crazy, and be afraid to
look Mama in the eye because of it.

"(Lyin in the fields all afternoon one afternoon,
watchin for the stallion to take the mare. It was fall and
the weeds were brown and live with seeds rattlin over
me. As I laid there I could hear the bellow of the bull in's
pen for Roma the cow out in the pasture. I waited and
waited and just about dark Good Lord it happened.
How the mare screamed and how the stallion leapt
with's hooves in the air like a great flyin horse of statues;
and I thought, 'I am as strong as this winged stallion but
nobody knows it and I will say nothin of it, keep it to
myself.' As I laid in the fields, somewhere in me I was
fillin with blood, and suddenly somewhere I was full
and throbbin with blood.)

"Then again, onct, in Shrevesport when we had all
moved there (it snowed and we were cold in our first
snow and Mama took all us kids ridin ever Sunday on

the streetcar to the end a line and back) and I was walkin
at night, and in a winda there in a jewelry store that I was
lookin in at in the rain suddenly there was an arm and a
white hand that reached down into the brightest winda
among all the glitterin diamonds and gold bands there
and then disappeared again. I stood and waited in the
rain till I was drenched, but no more white hand came
down again. (Some white hand to reach down! O reach
us out a hand; this hand has birds' blood on it, has a
crooked knuckle broken by a baseball hit out to me in
centerfield in a game at Charity when we played the
Bloomer Girls by that tomboy Sis Moody.) And then I
walked and walked in the rain that turned into snow and
I was drenched and frozen (but burnin); and walked
upon a park that seemed like the very patch of Hell
where there was couples whisperin, men to men and
men to women. Then I felt alone and lost in the world
with no home to go home to and I felt robbed of
everthing I never had but dreamt of and hoped I could
have; and then I thought, 'O I am young and have somethin to give and to be used.' But I had no memory of anything beautiful or of my own to call inside me to, to name
and touch; I could only go, in my mind through the
rooms of the house and find no one I could join with for
anything, or speak to; and I thought, 'I will return, then,
to my aloneness and fold back my secrets into it with me
and we will be folded together there in a secret and silent
place that will never be broken into, I will dive down

naked and alone into that place and touch what I never
had and hold it there, away from everbody on the outside of me.' (But he will break into my deep buried
place, I will let him break into me and then he will be
stained and marked by all my hidden secret and he will
touch and bring it up, saved, into the light and bind it to
everthing; for he belongs to everthing that ever was and
is. For what I'll put into him he cain't forget or wish
away, it is the truth of the world, and of walls, and of
men; and he must endure it and take it into hisself
willingly and keep it in the world, proclaim it.)

"O misery! I swear I never touched a woman or a
girl or anybody until it got to where I had to.

"At Daisetta, when I was stayin in the summer with
the Chanceys, me and Dave were in the yard when
Sarah, the biggest of us all, came out and just said, 'Do
you want to see me?' and showed us her beginnin
breasts, raw like a young sow's, and we went in the
house where nobody was and took turns feelin of em;
and then the little girl, Mary, came in and said, 'Want to
see mine?' and showed us where there was nothin at all
yet but shriveled places, like a man's. All that summer
Sarah was after us, cryin, 'You Merry Widows!'

"O Otey why did what happened have to happen? I
married you too young. She lived in a house way back in
some trees and was just a funny kind of bowed-over girl
(from carryin brothers and sisters on her hip) that hardly
ever came out of the trees into town, with a lot of the yel-

lowest cornsilky hair and a loose dress with no belt. Why
didn't they tell her that when we married I would want
to touch her? She screamed and ran from me that
wedding night out the door and down the rayroad tracks
and slipped on the ties and fell and cut over her eye that
left a scar like a shriveled apricot. She was a rabbit in the
house after I brought her back pantin and damp from
runnin, and bloody, and then I was dyin dyin to touch
her and could have almost killed her in my hands she
was so limp and little and white; but I said, 'All right,
little Otey, I'll wait for you, I'll wait until you grow up
big enough to be my wife.'

   "I was workin at the sawmill then, strawbossin the
niggers with the mules that pulled the logs from the kiln
to the plane, through the black sawdust in the mud, surrounded by the tearin sound of the cuttin of the logs, like
goods bein ripped all day long. I'd go home at dinner
and she'd have good butterbeans and peppersauce and
corn bread for me like I like and we'd eat and O Lord I'd
want to touch her but I wouldn't. Then they sent me out
to the Thicket with a crew to cut new timber and we
stayed there for a whole month and I would not touch
any niggers or any of the Indians that lived on the reser-
vation around there; and when I come back Otey was
gone. She had run home; and I let her stay; I didn't
blame her. I went home, back home, and Mama said,
'Here is where you belong, come on back to this house
with all of us.'

"I never told that I had never touched her — and no one ever knew. But I'll tell Boy, this little listener will listen, I'll tell him when the time comes.

"And then one day Sam Riddle come to say three girls swimmin in the river by White Rock had fallen in a deep hole and they had got two out but the third was drownded and would I come hep dive for the body of the third. I went with them and got to the river and they said to me the third one was Otey Bell. I took off all my clothes and dove in where they said she had sunk and went down down to China it seemed, prayin to touch Otey there, and in time; and Lord God I touched her. Then I opened my eyes quick and saw a sight I'll see in dreams until I die: Otey was sittin bent over with her head on her knees in some sorrow, and nekkid, and I grabbed her hair and crushed it in my hands for a second; and then I caught her hands with my hands and we were joined, just by our fingertips, so lightly, and came up slowly slowly. It was so long comin up, like a lifetime of Otey and me bein together in a darkness, alone and not sayin a word — but the bubbles of our breath were bathin us, we were wrapped in the bubbles of our breath, and they were our words speakin for us — and I prayed Lord Lord don't let me lose Otey, don't let me let her get away this time, because she had surrendered to me at last, she was mine, my wife now; and come up with me so quiet without fightin, and I was nekkid with her. Bubbles of her last breath rose and sprayed my loins and

clung to the hairs on me like diamonds breathed out by
her and we must have looked beautiful to fishes in our
underwater marriage, glitterin with diamonds of breath
and risin nekkid and touchin ever so lightly at our fingertips together, joined and flowin into each other, up to
the shore. As we rose up together all our life that we never had together happened within me — Otey cookin and
singin in our warm winter kitchen and me choppin
wood in the mornins. As we floated up through watery
vines and ferns and slippery roots through scales and
petals of sunlit water, layers breakin open over us as we
broke through them like thin leaves of silver, I
remembered that a hand does let down to you if you get
lonesome and lost enough, that a big broken
birdbloodied hand does reach down to you, wet and
alone and so lonesome; and that you are washed clean
by the touch of this hand. And as we came somethin
suddenly burst inside me and this was for love and for
Otey, drowned but rescued Otey. I did get to the top
with her and then those on the banks saw what it was
and Jim Moody yelled, 'Christy's found her,' and jumped in to help but I was nearly passed out and thought
they were tryin to take Otey away from me, and this time
it seemed she wanted to stay with me, even nekkid, and
I fought them off like a wilecat. Then Jim Moody hit me
hard up against the head and that was all I remember till
I woke up lyin out on the bank with the feelin of Otey's
fingertips on my fingertips. And I looked over to see the

three boys rollin poor Otey over a log to try to get the riverwater out of her lungs; but she was drowned dead.

"When I was young because I was big and big-handed they used me like a plowox — but I had in me the beautiful thing that could happen to me. Somethin is over us, flies over us always over us, and we must bring it down; somethin is under, down under, and we must bring it up for ourselves and for everbody.

"I was mean and wrong and unused until my one moment that lasted all my lifetime, it seemed, going down to find Otey — now I know what going down to find anything means: go *down*, Boy, after what is folded over like a child of sorrow, egg in its nest, and is all your life and love never had for your own, never owned but always waitin to embrace and hold warm to you, and *bring it up*, pullin it up with all the strength you've got in you to pull up anything with, holdin it just by your fingernails (that I bit them, once!), bring it up through all the darkness of the world, through all the circles of mizry, to the top and deliver it, though gone, though unbreathin and dead, retrieved and brought home to you where it has always belonged, to the rescuers of the perished on the shore. For below the level where we are nothin but nekkid murmurins and whisperins over the world, only breath breathin dialogues in bubbles: rememberin, and yearnin, grievin and desirin, we are the life that lasts in us and has its meanin in us all; we touch there where we can touch and join and enter into one another forever.

"We'll go to the cemetery, we'll go take flowers to the graves.

"O tell a child your griefs. Tell him all your wickednesses, all your secrets. Boy, Boy you are so good, what made you so good? I am spoiled and he is clean; O I am vile, a shitten lamb. I will corrupt him, do not let me corrupt him when we get to the thicket. I didn't spoil Otey, I let her wait; I can let a thing wait until it is time; O Lord, let me let him wait — but what will get him, what will claim him eventually and spoil him? Back a Shultzes Bakry onct, I drew a picture on the signboard of it and then took Hapabelle Cook back there to see it. But I never touched her. O myself, how splendid myself, good as a stallion, and pretty, and circumcised (is he?), for who, who got me? Does he do it? How will I ask him? (If your Uncle Jack was on a mule and couldn't get off would you help your Uncle Jack off?)"

We had come into the deepest gloom of the woods, vauted by enormous pinetrees, called the Thicket, and I knew it was time. I had a garland of birds Christy had shot and I had run to gather like flowers in a wild enchantment . . . How long had we been hunting? We were standing by a pool of the river. I looked at my quivering image in the pool, throbbing as if the pool were breathing through me. A purple snake glided over my image and Christy shot it, tearing my image into pieces.

And then he sat down on a stump (oh is that stump covered over with blooming vines now? do birds or possums nest in it?), looking as tired as if he had lived through all the ages, and with such a longing and such an ageing in his face that I backed away — for he looked like a beast in the woods, shaggy and gray and fierce. Yet some enormous tenderness was rising out of him. His look asked for something that I could not give because I had not learned how to give it.

I backed away, backed away and he sat still on the stump. He pointed his gun at me to shoot me like a bird; and I backed away. And then he lowered his gun and watched me and let me get away; and then I ran.

I ran and ran and felt myself melting down as I ran, but I would not cry. It was towards twilight and soon it would be dark. O which way was home? The sun was setting. I ran and ran.

All the woods were now saying the same things to me that I had heard during the long and timeless hunt with Christy. Something like stars was twinkling in my loins. I prayed. Moss hung from trees like long hair and I saw the little green fuzz on rocks. What would I ever do with all this that had been said to me, now that Christy knew I knew all this? I would pray against it. I walked praying through the woods. O which way was home? The sad dusk was falling, and I was lost, lost. There was a kind of purring of the woods before dark. Which way was home? I had left Christy alone in the woods and

night was coming. I called, "Christy Christy!" but only
the woods, faraway, called him too; and he did not
answer. Then I cried, "Christy Christy come home,
come ho-o-me!" Only an echo answered and no answer
from Christy came. Some burden weighed upon me,
some yoke around me.

I was by the river. There, in a place, I suddenly saw
the print of Christy's body in the sand where he had
kneeled down to drink, and I kneeled into it and drank
as Christy had and felt at that moment that I was Christy
drinking from our River. As I kneeled something swung
against my face like petals of flowers and it was the birds
Christy had shot and I had tied by their little legs to a
string, as fishermen do fish, and had strung them round
my neck. I saw that I was dappled by the blood of birds
and that the beaks had beaten against my bare arms as I
had run and brought my own blood there, mixed with
the blood of birds.

I ran on again with his yoke of birds swinging
against me, Christy's message to me. I ran blessed with
his yoke of loves, of words, his long sentence of birds,
bloody and broken and speechless, sentences of his language shot out of his air and off his trees' boughs that
were his words' vocabulary: flying words that call at
twilight and twilight, nest and hatch and fly free for others, yet caged in his birdcage of mind, and betraying
him, but freed by my hand on his hand; and brought
down solid and sullied by beebee shot from his air by

his own aim and fire (misfire!) for me to gather and make speak: answer to his caged whisper: with tongues of birds.

I ran marked and stained. How would I ever wash away all this blood of birds? O now he was bird and I was bird, he was my truth and my untruth, he was my victim, he contained me, I possessed him.

Now it was dark and I was full of fears. In a pond I passed, the moon lay fallen and small and mean among weeds and fallen branches. All birds were calling and returning to bough or nest without Christy there to try to shoot them, safe and homing at nightfall. O who would welcome me home when I finally got home?

Now the woods seemed a huge web that held Christy like a caught insect in it. Now I really *loved* Christy, longed for him, calling to him (O where was he?). We had come to the woods in a dream and in a quick dream he had faded away from me. The ripe cracking of his gunshot like the splitting of a ripe tree fired in my head. That I betrayed Christy! That I failed him in the woods, he who gave me all these gifts of birds, who spoke for the first time to me and waited for me to answer! To whom would I answer, to whom in the house would I answer when I came back, over the sea of bitterweeds of Bailey's Pasture riding in home, bottled news to be broken against the hands of the House that sealed the bottle? What he had put into me, through my eyes, through my ears, and marked and stained upon

my body was to be carried away, through the bit-
terweeeds, across the River and into the world to be read
out to the world. If I could only find him again to tell him
this, for he would want to know. I called his name into
the woods that he had called his own names into —
"Christy! Christy!" — but no answer came back, only
my own calling turned back into my ears.

   I was by the river and so tired with all the weight of
the birds. What would I ever do with them? And then I
knew . . . I flung them into the river. No one would ever
know. They went down, a flotilla of feathers, like a floating garden, like a wreath to the river drowned, for Otey,
for Christy, for all of us. I washed in the river. And then I
felt so light with all my burden and I lay down close to
the river's side, and slept.

   Suddenly I woke in touch with something, as forever after, in the air. Something called, something hovered, hard and real and whole as a soaring bird. *O
birdcursed, birdblessed, birddrenched* . . . He is all our Sin
and all our Vision and all our searching calling back to
us, claiming us. Just when I am free and clean and myself
again I hear this voice, I know this hovering — in my
ascensions like wings from a bough that I think are up
and away from him I am only soaring up to him — he is
my air, he receives me, I fly in him back to him.

   There is the river, over I must — across I'll go.

   It was morning and a new, known world. I walked

straight home and as I came through Bailey's Pasture, stained with all my stains and feathers in my hair and clinging to my clothes, the wind blew the feathers from me over the pasture and the feathers fell on the bitterweeds. Ahead, in the woodshed, I saw Christy sitting there and whittling. He did not even look up as I came through the gate and went into the house. In the house Malley was sitting by the window and Granny was nowhere to be found. No one even seemed to know that I had ever been away, and Christy never mentioned it. We never went hunting again.

Our winter was close and lay long and gray and leafless ahead. Something waited for me now — a world of magic and witchcraft in which there were secrets and dreams and fantasias, whirling in the glimmer of coming hope and hopelessness (who has not seen the gizzard-like birthmark on the luminous forehead of the moon?), and all of us speaking to each other, apart and solitary in our buried selves. All December the moon had a birthmark on it like Mrs. Childers the crazy woman had.

The coldest winter in anybody's memory came to Charity. All day some days there was the wild and savage howl of the wind loping round the house; and at night in the sleet the shivering brethren horses huddled against the wind. The wind was in the shutters, swing like a ghost the tire swing and rattled the cisternwheel.

Roma the cow got frozen in the ditch and Christy had to kill her. Granny sat below away from us in the cellar. Swimma was in Florida or somewhere; and Christy sat gazing at the map of the world in the kitchen or putting, wordlessly and patiently, the little ship in the turpentine bottle. I was listening to what everybody was saying and to what the blinded girl with the lyre on top of the world was singing; and our house was full of the breath of speech.

But our spring came and with it such thaws and such rains that there was the biggest flood in years and the river widened out even onto Bailey's Pasture and was so close to the house that we could see upon it drowned wooden cows rolling like barrels, lily pads of chickens floating and little outhouses and wagon-wheels. When the river finally shrank back to the bottomlands it had left in Bailey's Pasture crawfishes and catfish, pineneedles and spores and pinecones and its golden silt and the bones of birds; and it had taken back there with it bitterweeds and sawdust and go-to-sleep flowers and even the babybuggy that we had left in the pasture to be ruined by the worst winter.

XIII

SUDDENLY I was in touch with something, in the air. Something called, something hovered, hard and real and whole as a soaring bird. O Christy, our great lover! Reach down your birdbloodied hand to me, you who decorated me with your garland of news, crowned me with your birdbays of love, blessed me with the flowers and the songs of our woods, hung me with the trappings of our woods to send me, wrought like a frieze with all this beauty, all this knowledge, alone away through my inevitable journey away from you, like a new bird, fledged by your birdridden hands, towards home (O let me go!) to get there as I could and find my own and, for the first time, earned welcome, to learn the bitter parting that gives freedom and slavery; bless me now, unclaim me, haunt me, bless me now who led me away, broke my seal of secrets, then left me — violated and ready again: pattern of all the journeys I would ever make, bird-enchanted, bird-shadowed, bird-tormented . . .

For I am in those woods again where the dialogue of our shared secrets once flew like birds from the trees of your mind to the trees of mine (but there is a clearing ahead where the river turns and flows, cuts through the trees, shall I follow it?) where there seems and seemed to be no time, nor past nor future, where once I was lost for the first time away from the house and kin — homing! How homing? O home me! Where . . . ? — and thought of all of them, back there, Granny and Aunty and Malley and all the rest . . . Who am I, separated from all of them and from home, yet with the idea of them and the idea of home in my mind, claimed and cursed by these, blessed and marked, sent somewhere? Those who will ever see me naked will find upon my thigh the blue sign, the stigma but no blemish, really lovely, like a vein in an agate or the grain in wood — and they will know the touch of the birds upon me.

There is the river, over I must — across I'll go. For the vision burns away like cold blown breath; and when I look again it will have vanished away.

Christy make us real, make us hard and real in our lives: we who walk up and down in this autumn, trying to make ourselves real. We are involved, we are involved; and we cannot break away. All the history that we saw on the map in the kitchen pours into us and we contain it, we display it like a map for others to look at and be history; and the song of the girl on the world sings through us to be sung into others: *Go into the world, go build cities, go discover countries; go spread love, go give, go make magnificence, get and give light, save and join and piece together (as you did the bits of string and cloth and whittled wood to make your ship) and show a whole and put it, combined and formed and shaped, into the world like a bottle with a ship in it. Gather the broken pieces, connect them: these are the only things we have to work with. For we have been given a broken world to live in – make like a map a world where all things are linked together and murmur through each other like a line of whispering people, like a chain of whispers a full clear statement, a singing, a round, strong, clear song of total meaning, a language within language, responding each to each forever in the memory of each man.*

And then I said, "I will get up now and go now, where I belong, and be what I must be."

I went to the bus station and really waited for a bus this time, and took it, and the next morning I knew it was no spell when I heard them calling all the names of the little forgotten towns, Normangee, Sweetwater, Cheetah, and I saw the live oak trees like old kinfolks in the fields.

Then, after a while, I was in the road going to the house and looked up and there it was, on the little rising piece of land, waiting for me. Through the mist that lay between us it seemed that the house was built of the

most fragile web of breath and I had blown it — and that
with my breath I could blow it all away.

THE HOUSE OF BREATH

WILLIAM GOYEN   THE